HOPE SINGS!

SERMONS
ON THE
PSALMS

VOLUME 3

C. Anthony Hunt

C. Anthony Hunt

Hope Sings
Sermons on The Psalms
Volume 3
by C. Anthony Hunt

The Rhodes-Fulbright Library series

ALL RIGHTS RESERVED.

ISBN: 978-1-55605-525-6 Paperback

Ebook: 978-1-55605-526-3 E Book

WYNDHAM HALL PRESS

www.wyndhamhallpress.com

Printed in The United States of America

TABLE OF CONTENTS

C. Anthony Hunt

INTRODUCTION (The Introit)

Over time, I've come to realize that my preaching continues to be profoundly influenced by the imprint of music - especially music from the Black experience - and especially that of Aretha Franklin, Marvin Gaye, Donnie Hathaway, Roberta Flack, Stevie Wonder, Nina Simone, Anita Baker, Earth, Wind and Fire, Mahalia Jackson, Otis Redding, John Coltrane, Miles Davis, and Frankie Beverly and Maze, among others. It is their music that has been sources of inspiration and hope as expressed in the sermons in this volume, *Hope Sings!* From gospel to soul, rhythm & blues to jazz, and hip hop to reggae - I realize that music has been a lifeline for my preaching.

These are days in which we witness the precarious nature of hope, both in the church and society. As I have moved toward concluding writing this book, our nation and world continues to find itself in the grips of COVID-19, the worst health pandemic in our lifetime. This global health pandemic is married with the pandemics of racism and xenophobia, economic distress and political discord that continue to grip America. Indeed, these are days of perilous, precarious hope, and it is the churches and other faith communities that somehow must continue to speak and live hope, speak truth to power, seek peace with justice, and sing hope. Somehow, we must conjure the audacity, as the ancient prophet Joel intimated, "to see visions and dream dreams", and have the temerity to hope against all that seems to persistently rise against hope.

As is the case with each of my writing projects, this has been a communal experience. As always, I am grateful for my family that has continued to bring meaning, joy and hope to my life and work. I am forever grateful for Lisa, my wife, who continues to journey closely with me through life. To our children – Marcus (deceased), Kristen and Brian – I continue to be appreciative and proud of who God has made you to become. I am also thankful for our parents (and all of our ancestors), siblings and extended family.

Epworth Chapel United Methodist Church in Baltimore, Maryland, where I have been privileged to serve as pastor since 2011, continues to inspire me to become the very best pastor and leader I can be. I am grateful to be a co-laborer on the faith journey with this great church, which has been central in helping to shape all that is written in this volume. Similarly, to the places where I am privileged to teach – St. Mary's Seminary and University (Baltimore MD), Wesley Theological Seminary (Washington, DC), United Theological Seminary (Dayton, OH), and the Graduate Theological Foundation (Oklahoma City, OK) - I am thankful for all I continue to teach and learn in these institutions. I dedicate this volume to my family, congregants and students.

It is my prayer, as with my two preceding volumes of sermons on the psalms, *Keep Looking Up* (2016) and *Songs for the Seasons* (2020) - that this compilation of sermons will read like a songbook, speaking hope, and encouraging each who reads it to forever *sing hope!*

SECTION I
SONGS FOR UNCERTAIN TIMES
(SERMONS ON PSALM 23)

1. SONGS FOR UNCERTAIN TIMES –
WE NEED A SHEPHERD

The Lord is my shepherd, I shall not want. (Psalm 23:1)

So again, Jesus said to them, "Very truly, I tell you, I am the gate for the sheep. All who came before me are thieves and bandits; but the sheep did not listen to them. I am the gate. Whoever enters by me will be saved, and will come in and go out and find pasture. The thief comes only to steal and kill and destroy. I came that they may have life, and have it abundantly. "I am the good shepherd. The good shepherd lays down his life for the sheep. (John 10:7-11, NIV)

We begin this proclamation series on the psalms by recognizing that of all the psalms in scripture and all the songs that we've become accustomed to singing in and around the church over the years, the 23rd Psalm is the crown jewel of them all. It is the psalm that more people can recite than any other. The 23rd Psalm is not only a funeral psalm, but it speaks to many of life's vicissitudinous circumstances.

If we need assurance of God's presence, the 23rd Psalm is a psalm for us. If we need certainty of God's protection, this is our song. If we need assurance of God's peace, this psalm is the one. And if we need hope of God's provision, this psalm speaks to us.

And so, it is apropos that David sang this song for himself, for the believers of his day, and by extension, for us. How do we know that it was a song that David sang, first and foremost, for himself? We know because of how he began the song. He began by declaring that *"the Lord is MY shepherd."*

David did not say that the Lord is *OUR* shepherd, or *YOUR* shepherd, or *THEIR* shepherd, but he declared that *"the Lord is MY shepherd."* David placed his proclamation here in the context of the first-person, and who the Lord was to him.

Psalm 23:1 is David's personal affirmation of faith. It is his testimony, his praise song about who God was to him.

He declared that *"The Lord is MY shepherd."* And it is also apropos that David began this psalm by singing about who God is. Notice that he didn't start by singing about what God had done for him, but he started by saying that *"the Lord is my shepherd."*

This "ISNESS" speaks to the nature of God – the character and identity of God. I believe that it is more important now than ever that we know who is God, and know who God is not. For David to say that *"the Lord is my shepherd"* speaks to two things. *First, it speaks to the fact that God is a protector.* As God watched over and protected David, the same God will watch over and protect you and me. *"The Lord is our shepherd."*

What was David really trying to convey? If we were to have a conversation with David today, he might let us know that with everything he had gone through – with all the ups and downs in his life – with all the threats on his life, mistakes he had made - he could still testify that *"the Lord is my shepherd."*

David might tell us that "When I look back, and think about the times when I thought I wouldn't make it, when I thought I was alone, when I was broken and in need, I now realize that God was there." *"The Lord is my shepherd, and I shall not want... I don't need anything... I have everything I need."*

11

Second, David's declaration that "the Lord is my shepherd" speaks to the fact that if the Lord was his shepherd, then nobody else was. The reality for sheep is that sheep can only have one shepherd. There's only one shepherd that can call their sheep their own. Shepherds don't share sheep, and sheep cannot have more than one shepherd.

Many people today live thinking they have shepherds in other high places – in politics, in business, in the media, in sports, in entertainment, and even in church. But we all need to keep in mind that *all of us really only have one shepherd – that is God.* And even those of us who serve as pastors of churches are reminded that we are only under-shepherds to the *good shepherd* who is Jesus Christ.

This is the point that Jesus was making in John 10. There were those in his day who were not only wondering who he was, but wondering if God would protect them and be with them in the midst of what they were going through. Jesus stopped to remind them of who he really is. He said that *"I am the good shepherd."* Jesus was telling his followers that "In my "ISNESS", I will protect you and provide for you. *I am the good shepherd."*

"The thief comes to steal, kill and destroy. But I have come that you might have life, and have it abundantly" (John 10:10).

Indeed, we need a shepherd, and it's good to know that we have a *good shepherd* in Jesus Christ. Jesus will walk with us and talk with us, and tell us we're his own.

Sometimes when we're in an airport, we can observe the difference between passengers who hold confirmed tickets and persons who are on standby. Passengers with confirmed tickets may leisurely read newspapers, eat a snack, chat with their friends, or take a nap. Those on standby may hang around the ticket counter, and pace back and forth waiting for their name to be called. The difference is caused by the confidence factor.

Jesus, the *good shepherd*, the same Lord and shepherd that David sang about in Psalm 23, is our confidence factor as we walk by faith and not by sight. The Lord gives us confidence and comfort, provision and promise that he won't leave us or forsake us. As David walked through his valley of uncertainty, he had this confidence. And likewise, with whatever valleys of uncertainty might be our lot, we can walk with the same confidence that the Lord, our *good shepherd*, is with us along the way.

I've seen the lightning flash
And heard the thunder roll
I've felt sin's breaker's dashing
Which tried to conquer my soul.

I've heard the voice of my Savior
Telling me still to fight on
He promised never to leave me
Never to leave me alone.

2. SONGS FOR UNCERTAIN TIMES - LEAD US, LORD

He makes me lie down in green pastures; he leads me beside still waters. (Psalm 23:2)

Jesus answered her, "If you knew the gift of God, and who it is that is saying to you, 'Give me a drink,' you would have asked him, and he would have given you living water." The woman said to him, "Sir, you have no bucket, and the well is deep. Where do you get that living water? Are you greater than our ancestor Jacob, who gave us the well, and with his sons and his flocks drank from it?" Jesus said to her, "Everyone who drinks of this water will be thirsty again, but those who drink of the water that I will give them will never be thirsty. The water that I will give will become in them a spring of water gushing up to eternal life." (John 4:10-14)

As we arrive at the second verse of the 23rd Psalm, we find that David was making it plain to anybody who was paying attention the place that the Lord, his shepherd, had in his life. David used four action words in this second verse and the next verse to offer a depiction of what the Lord, his shepherd, did for him. He declared that the Lord: *(1) makes, (2) leads, (3) restores, and (4) guides.*

David was pointing to the fact that shepherds – by nature – have certain authority in their sheep's lives, and shepherds do certain things for their sheep. David knew something about shepherds because he had been one. Before he was called and anointed to be a king of Israel, David was a shepherd. Before he won great battles, and wrote many of the great worship songs that we know as psalms, David was a shepherd.

And so, David knew that sheep needed a shepherd to lead them to do certain things like rest in green pastures. He knew that shepherds knew how to lead their sheep to still waters. He knew that it was the role of shepherds to restore and encourage their sheep when sheep were weary and tired. David knew something about what a shepherd was supposed to do to guide their sheep because he had been one.

And the Lord was just like that for him. David knew that he could not lead himself. He knew that he could not make it on his own. He knew that he needed a shepherd. He knew that he needed the Lord to lead, restore and guide him.

Likewise, we need the Lord to lead us today. With every day's news, every strange tweet from national leaders, every derogatory and disparaging comment, with every act – for better or for worse - we see how important leaders are, and what leaders should and should not be, do and say.

Leadership consultant, John Maxwell has defined *leadership as influence – nothing more and nothing less.* Today, more than ever, we need the Lord to lead us and influence our lives.

Leadership is rooted in trust. In his role as a shepherd, David knew that his sheep had to have inherent trust in him. His sheep needed to be able to trust David with their lives. It's been said that when and if a leader loses the trust of their people, they lose their people.

And David knew from his own experience that he could not trust himself to lead himself in the right way. But he knew that he could trust God to put and keep him on the right path. He could trust God to keep him from going astray, and he could trust God to take care of him.

As I was growing up at St. Paul United Methodist Church in Oxon Hill, Maryland, there was a hymn that we would often sing in worship, "Lead Me, Guide Me":

Lead me, guide me... along the way.
Lord, if you lead me, I will not stray.
Lord, let me walk... each day with thee.
Lead me, O lord, Lead me.

Every time we would sing "Lead Me, Guide Me", I would sense the passion and deep yearning of the people of God, and our prayer that through whatever trials and tribulations we faced, whatever disappointments and despair we encountered, God would lead us and guide us, along the way.

And I'd sense the same when we would then sing Samuel Wesley's beautiful 19th century hymn, "Lead Me Lord":

Lead me, Lord, lead me in thy righteousness,
make thy way plain, before my face.
For it is thou, Lord, thou, Lord only,
that makest me dwell in safety.

Teach me, Lord, teach me truly how to live,
that I may come to know thee,
and in thy presence serve thee with gladness,
and sing songs of praise to thy glory.

Likewise, today it is God who we need to depend on to lead us in the right way. This was the point that Jesus was making with the woman at the well in John 4. She had tried a lot of things, been in a lot of places, and been in a lot of relationships. And now this Samaritan woman found herself in an unexpected encounter with Jesus. She had come to the well for water, but Jesus said, *"Everyone who drinks the water I will give them will never be thirsty again"* (John 4:14).

It is good news that Jesus looked beyond this woman's faults and saw her real needs. And it is good that what he did for this woman, he will do for you and me. He said, *"Let anyone who is thirsty come to me and drink. Whoever believes in me, as Scripture has said, rivers of living water will flow from within them"* (John 7:37-38).

One thing that Jesus showed us in his living, dying and resurrection is what a real leader does for his people. Jesus was hung on a cross and died for *all people.* Jesus was buried in a borrowed tomb *for all people.* Jesus was resurrected on the third day *for all people.*

A construction crew was building a new road through a rural area, knocking down trees as it progressed. A superintendent noticed that one tree had a nest of birds who could not yet fly, and he marked the tree so that it would not be cut down. Several weeks later the superintendent came back to the tree. He got into a bucket truck and was lifted up so that he could peer into the nest. The birds were gone. They had obviously learned how to fly.

The superintendent ordered the tree cut down. As the tree crashed to the ground, the nest fell out and some of the material that the birds had gathered to make the nest was scattered about. Part of it was a piece of paper torn from a Sunday school pamphlet. On the piece of paper were these words: *God cares for you.*

Be not dismayed
What e'er be tide
God will take care, of you.

17

C. Anthony Hunt

> *Beneath God's wings of love abide,*
> *God will take care of you.*
>
> *God will take care of you.*
> *Through every day, along the way,*
>
> *God will take care of you,*
> *God will take care of you.*
> *(Civilla Durfee Martin)*

3. SONGS FOR UNCERTAIN TIMES –
WHEN RESTORATION COMES

God restores my soul. God guides me along the right paths for God's name's sake. (Psalm 23:3)

Humble yourselves, therefore, under God's mighty hand, that God may lift you up in due time. Cast all your anxiety on God because God cares for you. Be alert and of sober mind. Your enemy the devil prowls around like a roaring lion looking for someone to devour. Resist him, standing firm in the faith, because you know that the family of believers throughout the world is undergoing the same kind of sufferings. And the God of all grace, who called you to God's eternal glory in Christ, after you have suffered a little while, will Godself restore you and make you strong, firm and steadfast. To God be the power for ever and ever. Amen. (1 Peter 5:6-11)

As we make our way to the 3rd verse of the 23rd Psalm, we find ourselves at a praise point for David, as he shared a couple of the things that God, his shepherd, did for him.

David declares that *the Lord restored his soul, and led him in the paths of righteousness for his name's sake.* Both of these matters - restoration and righteousness - spoke to David's spiritual life.

For, in as much as God had provided for him materially, in as much as God had made ways for David, he wanted those who were listening to know that among the most important things that God had done for him were to bless him spiritually, and watch after his soul.

And so, David here expressed his appreciation to the Lord for two spiritual blessings, *restoration and righteousness.*

David offered a testimony for being restored, and then being led along the path of righteousness.

What was Davis really saying? If we were to have a conversation with David, he might remind us that to be restored implies that there had been something that was out of alignment in his life.

We all face times in life when we need restoration. In another place in scripture, in Psalm 51, David prayed to God, *"Lord, restore unto me the joy of your salvation"* (Psalm 51:12).

Indeed, we all need to be restored at certain points in our lives - when life is unsettled - when our joy is lost - when our faith is shaken - when hope can't be found.

We need restoration when we can't love our neighbors (and enemies), when greed overtakes us, when life seems overwhelming. Indeed, we can all get to the place where David was when we need God to restore us. When was the last time you were like David and needed to be restored?

If we talked to David a little longer, he might also tell us that there are times when we find ourselves just going in the wrong direction in life, and needing to be put on the right path. God tells us to go left, and we go right. God says go right, and we go left.

There are times when our lives are like the cars we drive that get out of alignment, and we get out of alignment with God. We may find ourselves going in the wrong direction in life. We've all been there, haven't we? These are the times when we need the Lord to lead us in the paths of righteousness.

Furthermore, David might tell us that God does not just desire to bless our souls and make us right individually; that's not enough. God also wants to restore the soul of our communities, our nation and world, and put us on the right path toward becoming God's Beloved Community.

The nation and world are broken, and many of our communities and homes are broken - and the Lord, who is our shepherd, desires to restore us and make us right – bring us back into right relationship with God and with one another. About 2900 years ago, Solomon spoke a word for the Lord, *"If my people, who are called by my name, would humble themselves and pray, and turn from their wicked ways, I will hear from heaven, and heal the land"* (2 Chronicles 7:14).

In First Peter 5:10, the writer offers some words of encouragement to the church about restoration. The church in Peter's time was going through some things just like the church today. Peter, encouraged them with words of pastoral assurance that *"The God of all grace, who called you to God's eternal glory in Christ, after you have suffered a little while, will Godself restore you and make you strong, firm and steadfast"* (1 Peter 5:10).

In other words, restoration will come. It's good to know that *"trouble don't last always."* It's good to know that *"weeping may endure for a night, but joy comes in the morning"* (Psalm 30:5). It's good to know that *"the suffering of this present day is not worthy to be compared to the glory that will be revealed in us"* (Romans 8:18).

It's good to know that God specializes in restoration and righteousness. It's good to know that the Lord, our *good shepherd*, is in the business of performing reclamation projects - putting broken lives, broken relationships, broken communities, a broken nation and world back together again.

When a person works an eight-hour day and receives a fair day's pay for their time, that is a wage. When a person competes with an opponent and receives a trophy for their performance, that is a prize. When a person receives appropriate recognition for their long service or high achievements, that is an award. But when a person is not able to earn a wage, can win no prize, and deserves no award--yet receives such a gift anyway--that is a good picture of God's unmerited favor and blessing, God's grace.

That is why God sent God's only begotten Son, Jesus to earth. God looked down on creation, and realized that we needed a Savior to restore us and put us on the right path. He lived to restore us. Jesus died to make us right. And he rose from the grave on the third day to let us know that we've been redeemed. It's good to know that Jesus looked beyond our faults and saw all of our needs.

Amazing Grace shall always be my song of praise
For it was grace that brought me liberty.
I do not know just why God ever came to love me so
God looked beyond my faults and saw my need.

And I shall forever lift mine eyes to Calvary
To view the cross where Jesus died for me.
How marvelous the grace that caught my falling soul
God looked beyond my faults and saw my need.
(Dottie Rambo)

4. SONGS FOR UNCERTAIN TIMES - EVEN THOUGH

Even though I walk through the darkest valley, I will fear no evil, for you are with me; your rod and your staff, they comfort me. (Psalm 23:4)

On his arrival, Jesus found that Lazarus had already been in the tomb for four days. Now Bethany was less than two miles from Jerusalem, and many Jews had come to Martha and Mary to comfort them in the loss of their brother. When Martha heard that Jesus was coming, she went out to meet him, but Mary stayed at home. "LORD," Martha said to Jesus, "if you had been here, my brother would not have died. But I know that even now God will give you whatever you ask." Jesus said to her, "Your brother will rise again." Martha answered, "I know he will rise again in the resurrection at the last day." Jesus said to her, "I am the resurrection and the life. The one who believes in me will live, even though they die; and whoever lives by believing in me will never die. Do you believe this?" (John 11:17-26)

As we arrive at verse 4 of Psalm 23, we find ourselves at the place where David is reflecting on the low places in which he had found himself in life - the proverbial valley times and dark places of life.

Here, David turned his song into a first-person conversation with God as to where God had been in his valley times. Where in the first three verses of the 23rd Psalm, David sang to others about God, giving them a third-person account about who God is, and what God had done for him, here in the

23

fourth verse, he talked directly to God, about *God's presence, God's proximity in his life.*

David said, *"Even though I walk through the darkest valley, I will fear no evil, for you are with me; your rod and your staff, they comfort me."*

His depiction here was one of walking through a *"valley of the shadow of death."* Some commentators have characterized this valley as *Death Valley* - like the *valley of dry bones* that the prophet Ezekiel said that he had been set down into some 200 years after David wrote his song.

We can imagine that David's reflections here placed him in the existential place of darkness, depression, despair and death - a low place in his life. This is the spiritual condition that John of the Cross referred to as *"the dark night of the soul."*

We've all been there, haven't we? We've all had to endure low points in life. Valley experiences, dark places are a part of all of our testimony. Low points - when depression and death meet us, when sickness and sorrow greet us, when trials and tumult threaten to defeat us.

Valley situations will come our way. There will come points when relationships break, when disappointment, discouragement and disconsolance enter into our lives. We've all been there, haven't we?

And valley experiences and dark places are not confined to us individually. We see that our nation and world are in the midst of a valley - with economic despair for too many, social decay among us and political discord that is pervasive. We find valleys in many of our communities - with distress, tragedy and violence in too many places.

If we just turn on the television or open an Internet browser, we will see that in too many ways we are living in a valley like the one David was talking to God about in Psalm 23:4.

And so, what does this seminal fourth verse in Psalm 23 have to say to us today about where we find ourselves individually and communally?

For an answer, we might listen to what Dave had to say in the text. As we look closely at the text, we notice that he began verse 4 with two important words - *"Even though"*. Those two words indicate that whatever has gone on before is not the end, but that something else - perhaps something better and greater - is about to happen. David began verse 4 with *"Even though."*

Some of us might find ourselves in an *"even though"* place in life right now. *Even though* life seems to be a wreck, *even though* our finances may be in disarray, *even though* sickness might persist, *even though* we're walking in a particular valley right now, we're not afraid because we believe, as David did, that *God is with us; God's rod and staff comfort us.*

Making our way to John 11:17, we find that Mary and Martha found themselves in an *even though* place in their lives. Their brother, Lazarus had died, and they were looking for Jesus, the one in whom they had put their faith and trust. *Even though* Jesus didn't show up when Mary and Martha wanted him to, he did show up. And when the Lord showed up, he reminded them that not only would their brother, Lazarus, be resurrected, but that Jesus is the *resurrection and the life.*

It's good to know that Jesus meets us in the *"even though"* times and places of life. It's good to know that God brings us through the valley situations that we find ourselves in.

There is a story from a professional football game from a number of years ago between the New York Giants and the

25

Chicago Bears. During the game, a television commentator shared the observation that over his long career, Hall of Fame running back Walter Payton had run the football for over 9 miles. The sports commentator then added that what that means is that Walter Payton got knocked down every 4.6 yards, and got back up and did it again in the equivalence of a 9-mile, multi-year run.

Isn't it good to know that every time we get knocked down in life, God will pick us up, and give us the strength to do it again? God gives strength to the weary to run on to see what the end will be.

At Calvary, they hung Jesus on an old rugged cross. He hung on the cross for three hours - suffered, bled and hung his head and died. They buried Jesus in a borrowed tomb. And on the third day he rose from the dead. And Jesus, *the resurrection and the life,* got up so that we can get up, and get through whatever trials and tribulations may come our way!

Because He lives, I can face tomorrow
Because He lives, all fear is gone
Because I know He holds the future
And life is worth the living, just because He lives.
(Bill Gaither)

5. *SONGS FOR UNCERTAIN TIMES - THROUGH*

Even though I walk through the darkest valley, I will fear no evil, for you are with me; your rod and your staff, they comfort me. (Psalm 23:4)

An analysis of the book of Psalms indicates to us that it is a book for all seasons of our lives. For every predicament and peril, and for every point of progress and possibility in life - there is one of the 150 divisions of psalms that speaks to it.

For the Israelites, the Psalms were like unto the great Stevie Wonder's seminal 1976 album, "Songs in the Key of Life". The psalms were their *"songs in the key of life."*

Through every trial and tribulation, there was a song. Through every triumph, there was a song. Through every one of their ups and downs, there was a song. Through all of their joys and pains, they sang. And among all of the psalms, many Christians and persons of other faiths around the world, over the ages, have found Psalm 23 to be the song that lives with us the most. It is not unusual for persons to be able to recite this particular psalm.

David's experience as depicted in Psalm 23 has, in many ways, become our experience. For those who are lonely, David's words serve as a comfort and companion. For the hurting, his words serve as a healing balm. For those in despair, David's song is one of hope for us.

And it is in the middle of David's six-verse song that is Psalm 23, that we arrive at the point where we find that David offers us an affirmation of his faith, and shares these most memorable words:

"Even though I walk through the darkest valley, I will fear no evil, for you are with me; your rod and your staff, they comfort me."

For a few moments, I invite us to park at one word found in verse four of Psalm 23. That word is *"through."*

"Even though I walk through the darkest valley, I will fear no evil..."

Here, David described his own *going through* as a valley experience. In fact, it was not just any valley that David was *going through* - he called it the "valley of the shadow of death," the "darkest valley."

We don't know exactly what David was referring to here, but we do know he was talking about having *gone through* the darkest of valleys – a dark place and time in his life.

Indeed, most of us can relate to David's *going through*. Each of us has *gone through* some things, is *going through* something, and will *go through* some things at some points in life in the future. And when we are *going through* things, it can become easy to feel that we are "too through," that we are "stuck", or that we want to give up, give in, throw in the towel, tap out and quit on life.

So, what might we learn from David's *going through* to help us with whatever we might *go through* today and tomorrow?

- First, *if we are going through, we are not stuck.* If we are living and breathing, we can give God thanks and praise because God is not finished with us. Indeed, it's good to know that God is not done with us.

28

- Second, *if we are going through*, and if we are walking by faith and not by sight, *we are not going through alone.* David's affirmation of faith is *"Lord, you are with me; your rod and staff, they comfort me."* Indeed, faithful people believe that God is with us with whatever we are *going through.*

- Third, *if we are going through, we'll have a testimony and doxology of praise when God brings us out.* What was David's doxology? We need to make our way to verse 6 of Psalm 23 to hear David's praise offering after *going through* and God bringing him out of his valley situation – *"Surely, goodness and mercy will follow me all the days of my life, and I will dwell in the house of the Lord forever."*

We may be *going through*, but thank God, we're not *going through* alone.

We may be *going through*, but it's good to know that we have *God's grace and mercy to carry us and bring us through.* We may be *going through*, but we know that with God, we're coming out!

Ask the Savior to help you,
Comfort, strengthen and keep you.
He is willing to help you,
Jesus will carry you through.
(H. R. Palmer)

6. SONGS FOR UNCERTAIN TIMES - GOOD AND PLENTY

You prepare a table for me in the presence of my enemies. You anoint my head with oil; my cup overflows. (Psalm 23:5)

Jesus said to them, "Very truly I tell you, it is not Moses who has given you the bread from heaven, but it is my Father who gives you the true bread from heaven. For the bread of God is the bread that comes down from heaven and gives life to the world." "Sir," they said, "always give us this bread." Then Jesus declared, "I am the bread of life. Whoever comes to me will never go hungry, and whoever believes in me will never be thirsty." (John 6:32-35)

I'm needy! We're needy! This message is for some needy people.

Certainly, one of the most important primary attributes and properties of God is that *God is a provider of all the things that we need. God is omni-benevolent – all-giving and all-good.* This matter of provision speaks to our most basic needs in life. Indeed, a part of being human is coming to grips with the fact that we all have physical, social and spiritual needs. We're needy. And a corollary to this realization is that we can't meet all of our needs on our own.

David had arrived at this realization in Psalm 23:5. He had come to the point in life where God had delivered him – brought him out of the dark place where he had found himself. God had led him through and out of a valley of darkness and despair that he had experienced and walked through (Psalm

23:4), and as God had brought him out, he now wanted to share something with God in a prayer.

David said, *"Lord, you prepare a table for me in the presence of my enemies."* Isn't it interesting that as God brought David out, God didn't just bring him out of his situation and leave him alone to fend for himself? But when God brought David out, God brought him out and then provided for him.

And so, we can surmise from David's experience and testimony that God never brings us out of a situation without providing for us in our new destination.

And furthermore, we are reminded that even in our new destination, our enemies will meet us there. Indeed, wherever we go, we may encounter enemies. David said to the Lord, *"You prepare a table for me in the presence of my enemies."*

What's an enemy? An enemy is anybody who doesn't have our best interests at hand. An enemy is anybody who wants to do us harm.

Even as David had come out of his dark valley situation, Psalm 23:5 implies that there were enemies waiting to take him out or take him into another valley. But what David declared is that in the midst of this, God had prepared a table for him in the presence of his enemies. It's good to know that God's goodness and provision supersede the evil and hatred that our enemies might want to inflict on us.

Indeed, God shows up in the presence of our enemies to let us know that God is greater than our adversaries and adversity, and that nothing that we will encounter is too hard for God to handle.

Enemies, adversaries and adversity might come our way, enemies might loom large at points in our lives, but we rest in the blessed assurance of knowing that God is greater. That is why Joseph could declare that *"what you meant for evil, God meant if for good"* (Genesis 50:20).

That is why Isaiah could declare in the midst of adversity all around him and God's people, that *"no weapon formed against you shall prosper"* (Isaiah 54:17). That is why John could declare that, *"greater is God that is in you than he that is in the world"* (1 John 4:4).

Those who came to Jesus in John chapter 6 were likewise needy. They came to the Lord because they were hungry, and they expected the Lord to provide physical food. Jesus already had a history of providing for needs as he ministered through Galilee. He was known to heal the sick and raise the dead. He was known to provide water for the thirsty, and had already fed the hungry. In fact, just a day before this encounter in John 6, Jesus had taken two fish and five loaves of bread, and he had fed over 5,000 people.

But the people wanted more physical food. They wanted Jesus to feed them again. Here in John 6, Jesus paused to remind the people that he not only came to give them physical food, but he came to give them life. Jesus not only provided bread, but he let them know that he is the *"bread of life"*.

And as it was for people over 2000 years ago, God in Christ not only feeds us and provides for our physical needs today, but God is the source that will give us eternal life.

When I was growing up, we had an afterschool ritual that carried over into our teen years. Almost every day at about 3:00 in the afternoon, we could expect a bell to start ringing outside in our neighborhood. On the corner, the Candy Man would drive up and park his truck, and we would all run outside, line up at the truck and spend our quarters or $.50 on the candy of our choice. Sometimes I'd buy *"Now or Laters"*, sometimes I'd buy *M and M's,* and every now and then, I'd buy *Good and Plenty*.

The packaging for *Good and Plenty* was a reminder that *what was inside was not only "good", but it was "plenty".* Isn't that what God is for us, *"good" and "plenty"?* Isn't that the way God provides for us, *"good" and "plenty"?*

David concluded this fifth verse of Psalm 23 by declaring with a praise offering, *"my cup overflows."*

It's good to know that God provides for us, *"good" and "plenty".* It's good to know that because of God's provision, our cups overflow.

The song-writer declared, *"all (not some, but all) I have needed, your hand has provided! Great is God's faithfulness!*

7. SONGS FOR UNCERTAIN TIMES –
GOD'S ANOINTING MAKES THE DIFFERENCE

You prepare a table for me in the presence of my enemies.
You anoint my head with oil; my cup overflows. (Psalm 23:5)

The Spirit of the Lord is on me, because God has anointed me
to proclaim good news to the poor. God has sent me to
proclaim freedom for the prisoners and recovery of sight for
the blind, to set the oppressed free, to proclaim the year of the
Lord's favor. (Luke 4:18-19)

One of the realities of how God has created us, and a
reality of the human condition is that we all have needs that are
more profound and pronounced than our material needs.
Certainly, we need material things in order to survive. We need
food and water. We need clothing and shelter, and we need
some means of providing for our loved ones. We need people
in our lives to support us, encourage us and love us. These are
the things that we can see and feel.

But we all need more. We all yearn to connect with God
on a deeper, spiritual level. This is what makes us complete.
St. Augustine, the fourth century Bishop of Hippo, reminded us
of our human need to connect with God in a prayer, *"Lord, you*
have created us for yourself, and our souls are restless until
they find their rest in you."

This is where David found himself as we make our way
to Psalm 23:5. First, he shared that *"God had prepared a table*
for him in the presence of his enemies." In other words, God

had provided for David… God had made ways for him, and had been on-time in coming to see about David.

But as David moved to the second half of this fifth verse, he shifted his focus from what God had done for him materially to what God had done for him spiritually. David said, *"Lord, you anoint my head with oil; my cup runs over."*

Anointing was familiar to David and the people of Israel, as it was a part of their ritual (religious) life. Anointing was done by either smearing or pouring, and usually involved the use of water or oil.

Historically anointing had three purposes. It was used as a means of health and comfort, as a token of honor, and as a symbol of consecration. We remember that David was anointed by Samuel as he was identified and consecrated to succeed Saul as king of Israel.

Fundamentally, anointing was a sign of God's presence, God's favor, blessing and grace in people's lives. It was evidence that the Spirit of the Lord was present in, on and among them.

Indeed, in order for our lives to be complete, we need God's anointing. *God's anointing makes the difference in our lives.* In the 1950's Dr. Martin Luther King, Jr. preached a sermon entitled, "Three Dimensions of a Complete Life."

In the sermon, King indicated that in order for our lives to be complete, we need to have *length, breadth and height* in our lives. The *length* of our lives is measured by what we achieve from the point of our birth to our earthly death. But length alone is not enough for a complete life.

We also need *breadth* in life. The *breadth* of our lives is measured by the quality of our relationships with others. Indeed, we need each other to survive and be complete. As John Don intimated in a poem years ago, "No man is an island."

The *breadth* of our lives is also measured by our service with, to and for others. King intimated that "all of us can be great because all of us can serve." But length and breadth alone don't make a complete life.

We also need *height* in our lives. The *height* of our lives pertains to how high we ascend in our relationship with God, the quality of our spiritual life. It points to the notion that *God's anointing makes the difference in our lives.*

Indeed, if we've ever needed God's anointing in our lives, we need it now. We need the anointing in our individual lives, in our communities, in the church, and in the nation and world.

In Luke 4, Jesus entered the synagogue, opened the scroll to Isaiah 61, and started preaching. Jesus said:

"The Spirit of the Lord is on me,
  because God has anointed me
  to proclaim good news to the poor.
God has sent me to proclaim freedom for the prisoners
  and recovery of sight for the blind,
to set the oppressed free,
to proclaim the year of the Lord's favor."
(Luke 4:18-19)

Jesus knew that he couldn't do anything without God's anointing in his life. So, he began by proclaiming that *"The Spirit of the Lord is on me."* Jesus was concerned for the poor, the imprisoned, the blind, and the oppressed. And he knew that he needed God's anointing to minster and proclaim good news to those on the margins of society.

Jesus knew that he couldn't heal the sick without God's anointing. He knew that he couldn't raise the dead without

God's anointing. He knew that he couldn't feed the hungry or walk on water without God's anointing. Jesus knew, as Isaiah knew some 600 years earlier, that *God's anointing makes the difference.*

We likewise can rest assured that God's anointing makes the difference in our lives.

> *Spirit of the living God, fall fresh on (us).*
> *Spirit of the living God, fall fresh on (us).*
> *Melt (us), mold (us)*
> *Fill (us), use (us).*
> *Spirit of the Living God, fall fresh on (us).*
> *(Daniel Iverson)*

God's anointing makes the difference in our lives!

8. SONGS FOR UNCERTAIN TIMES – "SURELY!"

Surely your goodness and mercy will follow me all the days of my life, and I will dwell in the house of the LORD forever. (Psalm 23:6)

The elder, To the lady chosen by God and to her children, whom I love in the truth - and not I only, but also all who know the truth - because of the truth, which lives in us and will be with us forever: Grace, mercy and peace from God the Father and from Jesus Christ, the Father's Son, will be with us in truth and love. (2 John 1:1-3)

It is not an overstatement to declare that the times in which we now live are some of the most uncertain times that most of us, if not all of us, can remember, and had lived through. It might sound a bit nostalgic, but in days past, we could be almost certain of some things. We could count on there being relative safety in our homes, communities, schools and churches. We could place our trust in certain authority figures – politicians, minsters, teachers and public safety officials. We could be relatively certain that if people made promises to us, they would follow through and keep their promises, and that most – if not all - of what persons told us would be true.

Now uncertainty abounds. We're uncertain about our individual lives, our communal lives and the world around us. We awaken, day-by-day, to uncertainty as to whether the world will change with the flick of a switch, or with another terrorist attack. We're uncertain about who's telling the truth, and who's not. Indeed, uncertainty abounds.

As we arrive at the final verse in Psalm 23, David found himself at a point of doxology and praise. In this capstone of the psalms, David spent the first five verses extolling the attributes of God – his shepherd. He acclaimed how God had protected and provided for him, how God had guided, led, restored, delivered and anointed him. And David concluded by declaring with words of praise to God, *"Surely, goodness and mercy will follow me all the days of my life, and I will dwell in the house of the Lord forever."*

This was another affirmation of faith for David. *"Surely!"* Not maybe, or perhaps, but David declared, *"Surely"*, God's goodness and mercy would follow him. No conjecture or wonder resided with David here. He was able to finally declare, *"Surely!"*

How could David have arrived at a point of *"surely"* in his life? It's easy to see that as David sketched his life through the first five verses of Psalm 23, he had grounds to have arrived at his *"surely."* After all that David had gone through, after all that God had brought him though, after every way that God had made, and after every table that God had set for him - all David could declare was *"Surely".*

After every mountain God had brought him over, and every valley God had seen him through, David could declare *"Surely."* David had a certain certainty. He had an assurance that if God had blessed him so mightily in the past, God would *"surely"* bless him mightily in the future, all the days of his life.

But I suspect that David wasn't just singing about his *"surely"* for himself, or for God. For God already knew what God had done for David, and David already knew what the Lord had done for him. So, we might ask, "Why else might David have sung about his *"surely"*? David might have sung about his *"surely"* to remind us today that each of us has a *"surely"* about which we can testify.

Your *"surely"* might not be my *"surely"*, but we all have one. When we look back over our lives, and think things over, we can all declare that *"Surely"*, God has healed. *"Surely"*, God has made ways out of no way. *"Surely"*, God has shown up on time. *"Surely"*, God has forgiven us. *"Surely"*, God has turned our lives around.

What's your *"surely"*? Every now and then, we should take a praise break, and let God know what God has *"surely"* done for us.

David's *"surely"* was that *God's goodness and mercy would follow him all the days of his life, and that he would dwell in God's presence forever.*

One Sunday, the young people in church were asked to define "mercy". Several of the young people gave very profound and accurate definitions of what mercy is. One response was particularly profound and striking. The young person said that *"Mercy is when God cuts us some slack."*

We can all thank God for "cutting us some slack." We can thank God for mercy in looking beyond our faults and seeing our needs. We can thank God for offering us unconditional love and forgiveness that covers a multitude of our faults, frailties and failures.

And we can thank God for grace in blessing us in ways that we don't always deserve. We can thank God for favoring our lives in ways that are unmerited. We can thank God for *demonstrating God's love toward us in that while we were yet sinners, Christ died for us* (Romans 5:8).

We can thank God for seeing us through many storms, dangers, snares, toils, trials and tumult in life. Not long ago, I had a plane flight from Miami to Baltimore. About two-thirds of the way through the flight, the plane started to experience serious turbulence, and we who were passengers started to shake in our seats. The pilot announced that he was turning on the fasten seatbelt sign for the remainder of the flight. For the rest of the flight, the plane shook from side to side. I was sitting near one of the airplane's wings, and noticed that even the wing looked like it was shaking.

As we approached the landing strip, the plane kept shaking, everybody on the plane was quiet, and some of us were holding on, expecting a rough landing. The pilot was able to make a smooth landing, and suddenly it was as though we hadn't gone through any turbulence at all. All I could do is testify, and declare that *"Surely"* it was God's grace and mercy that was with us through the turbulence of our flight, and brought us to a smooth, safe landing. And, as the psalmist declared in another place, *"if it had not been for the Lord who was on our side, where would we have been"* (Psalm 124:1).

Sometimes, we have to go through turbulence in life in order to realize that it is God who has brought us through, and allowed us to land smoothly. There are points in all of our lives on which we can look back and declare – *"Surely", God's goodness and mercy has been with us, and that same goodness and mercy will follow us all the days of our lives.*

Blessed assurance, Jesus is mine!
Oh, what a foretaste of glory divine!
Heir of salvation, purchase of God,
born of his Spirit, washed in his blood.

This is my story, this is my song,
praising my Savior all the day long.

C. Anthony Hunt

> *This is my story, this is my song,*
> *praising my Savior all the day long.*
> *(Fannie Crosby)*

SECTION II
SONGS OF ENCOURAGEMENT

9 - IT'S A LOVE THING

I will sing of your steadfast love, O LORD, forever; with my mouth I will proclaim your faithfulness to all generations. I declare that your steadfast love is established forever; your faithfulness is as firm as the heavens. You said, "I have made a covenant with my chosen one, I have sworn to my servant David: I will establish your descendants forever, and build your throne for all generations." Selah. (Psalm 89:1-4)

As we give careful consideration as to who God is, we constantly arrive at the point where we see and know that *God is love*. All that God is and is to be is rooted in divine love. All that God has done, is doing and will do is rooted in divine love.

God created the world, and all living things out of divine love. God created you, me and all of humanity out of divine love.

The psalmist knew of God's love, and declared so with these lyrics: *"I will sing of your steadfast love, O LORD, forever; with my mouth I will proclaim your faithfulness to all generations"* (Psalm 89:1).

Indeed, the psalmist had intimate knowledge and experience with the love of God. He knew God's love to be steadfast. It is one thing to know about love, and to be able to sing about love – and it is yet another thing to know about God's steadfast love.

For the psalmist to sing about the steadfast love of God, was to sing about God's loving consistency in his life. It was to sing about the fact that God's love is immutable, unchanging and had been with him through all of the vicissitudinous episodes of his life – through ups and downs, through joys and pains, through sunshine and rain, in better and in worse, in sickness and sorrow. He could testify that God's love had been steadfast and consistent in life.

Some of us are like the psalmist, and we could take a praise break at any moment and sing of God's steadfast love in our lives. We are like the psalmist with our testimony that God's grace and mercy have been consistent in our lives. We can testify that God's lovingkindness has been better to us than life. When everything around us has seemed to have given sway, when our world has been rocked and riveted by the restless seas of time, we can likewise testify that God's love has been steadfast and consistent.

For the psalmist, and for many of us, to consider how God has worked in our lives is to declare that *it's a love thing.*

In 1979, the soul singing group, the Whispers, sang about a love thing. They sang:
It's a love thing, it's a love thing –
every time that you're near,
it becomes so clear,
it's a love thing.

The Whispers were singing about a love interest, but they could have just as easily been singing about God's steadfast love - *"... every time that you're near... it becomes so clear... (God), it's a love thing."*

Just as the Whispers sang of their love interest, we need to know that God's love interest is you, me and all of humanity. God whispers in each of our ears, and reminds us that for God, *it's a love thing.*

In fact, God loved us so much that some 2000 years ago, God looked down on humanity and decided to send God's only begotten Son into the world so that we might have life.

God loved us so much that God sent Jesus into the world not to condemn us, but that through Jesus we would be saved. God loves so much that God sent a Son and a Savior for us. *It's a love thing.*

It is the divine love that St. Augustine prayed to God about some 1600 years ago: *"(Lord) You have created us for yourself, and our souls are restless until they find rest in you".*

The great Nobel Laureate Toni Morrison intimated that *"love is or it ain't. Thin love ain't love at all."* Many of us can testify to the fact that *God's love is, and it is thick.* It is steadfast, consistent, and persistent in our lives.

It is the divine love that Howard Thurman wrote of in his Christmas reflections:

"Behold the miracle! Love has no awareness of merit or demerit; it has no scale by which its portion may be weighed or measured. It does not seek to balance giving and receiving. Love loves: this is its nature."

Thurman had it right. *"Love loves: this is its nature."* As the psalmist knew and sang about, God's steadfast love loves us steadfastly, unconditionally, consistently, persistently and in all-abounding, everlasting ways. *It's a love thing.*

God's love is a love supreme. John Coltrane intimated such in the liner notes of his great 1964 song, "A Love Supreme":

(God's) way – it is so lovely – it is gracious.
It is merciful – thank you God.
One thought can produce millions of vibrations.
And they all go back to God... everything does.

We can rest in blessed assurance and holy certainty that God, in steadfast love - sees and knows all that we are going through. We can abide in confidence and hope that God in steadfast love knows and cares about our struggles and strengths, our trials and triumphs, our valleys, vicissitudes and victories.

We can rest assured that God in-flesh, incarnate, in Christ *knows all about our troubles, and God won't rest until the day is done.*

Yes, Howard Thurman was right. *"Love loves: that is its nature."* Toni Morrison was right. *"Love is or it ain't. Thin love ain't love at all."*

The psalmist in his moment of praise and appreciation about the love of God said –

"I declare that your steadfast love is established forever; your faithfulness is as firm as the heavens" (Psalm 89:2). Indeed, he knew something about God's love.

- God's love is abundant and audacious - bold and beautiful.
- God's love is committed and contagious - dutiful and delightful.
- God's love is excellent and excessive - fierce and forever.
- God's love his graceful and glorious - heaven-sent and hope-filled.

God's love will never lose its power. It reaches to the highest mountains and flows through the lowest valley.

God's love will never lose its power.
- It came wrapped in flesh.
- It heals, delivers and feeds.
- It forgives, saves and sanctifies.

Jesus is the embodiment of God's love, a love supreme. Jesus said, "There is no greater love than to lay down one's life for one's friends" (John 15:13). Because of such love, he died on a rugged cross for us, was buried in a borrowed tomb for us, and rose on the third day for us.

I was sinking deep in sin
Far from the peaceful shore
Very deeply stained within
Sinking to rise no more
But the Master of the sea
Heard my despairing cry
From the waters lifted me,
Now safe am I.

Love lifted me
love lifted me
when nothing else would help
love lifted me.
(Alan Jackson)

10 - A LIMITLESS LOVE

I have a message from God in my heart concerning the sinfulness of the wicked: There is no fear of God before their eyes. In their own eyes they flatter themselves too much to detect or hate their sin. The words of their mouths are wicked and deceitful; they fail to act wisely or do good. Even on their beds they plot evil; they commit themselves to a sinful course and do not reject what is wrong. Your love, LORD, reaches to the heavens, your faithfulness to the skies. Your righteousness is like the highest mountains, your justice like the great deep. You, LORD, preserve both people and animals. How priceless is your unfailing love, O God! People take refuge in the shadow of your wings. They feast on the abundance of your house; you give them drink from your river of delights. For with you is the fountain of life; in your light we see light. Continue your love to those who know you, your righteousness to the upright in heart. May the foot of the proud not come against me, nor the hand of the wicked drive me away. See how the evildoers lie fallen— thrown down, not able to rise! (Psalm 36:1-12)

If you know like I know, there's a lot of hate and hatred going on in our world today. We see, hear and feel hate all around us – on the television, on social media, in many of our social interactions. Hate and hatred are all around us.

Hate is clearly seen in the things that divide the human family – the "isms" and "phobias" that create relational fault lines among us – racism and sexism, classism and militarism, terrorism and denominationalism, traditionalism and tribalism.

We see and experience hatred in the fault lines of xenophobia, homophobia and Islamophobia.

We see and experience hatred among ourselves in how we relate (or fail to relate) with people who don't look like us, sound like us, believe like us, dress like us, worship like us, go where we go, or agree with us.

These fault lines among us result in the social and spiritual tsunamis that we now find ourselves in as a nation, world, and even, in some ways, as the Christian family. These fault lines result in division, discord and strife among us.

In the midst of all of this then, we might ask – *where is the love?* For, we know that love is the antithesis of hate and hatred. We know that *God is love* (1 John 4:7). We know that *"God so loved the world that God sent God's only begotten Son into the world"* to save us and give us new life (John 3:16). We know that *"God demonstrated God's love toward us in that while we were yet sinners, Christ died for us"* (Romans 5:8).

We have heard, and we know all of this about the love of God, and still the question today is, "where is the love of God in the midst of the hate around us?"

When we have questions about important life matters like this, one of the best places to turn is to the psalms. For, it is in the psalms that we find songs for all occasions, all seasons of life – songs of joy and sorrow; songs of striving and searching; songs of thanksgiving and celebration. And so, we can look to the psalms to the find an answer to the question of where the love of God might be located amidst the muck and mire of our world today.

And we find an answer in Psalm 36. The psalmist declared in verse 5 of this song that *"(Lord), your love is in the heavens; your faithfulness reaches to the skies".* In other words, the love of God is not conditioned on our human limitations, on whether we love one another or not, or even by whether or not we love God. God's love is a limitless love – God's "love is in the heavens, and God's faithfulness reaches to the skies."

With this affirmation of his faith, we can surmise that the psalmist was not unlike you and me. He must have spent some time wondering about where God's love was located in his life. Maybe there was some hatred in his midst. Maybe there were some unloving people in his life.

And so, the psalmist declared, Lord, *"Your love is in the heavens."* And he didn't stop with verse 5; he went on to sing about God's love two more times in this song. In verse 7, he sang, *"How priceless is your unfailing love, O God!"* And again, in verse 10, he sang, *"Lord continue your love to those who know you."*

It's good to know that God's love is a limitless love. This psalm isn't for those who have never experienced any hate, nor is it for those among us who have always been able to locate and experience God's love.

This psalm is for those of us who need to be reminded every now and then that God's love is a limitless love. God's love reaches to those who are White, Brown and Black. God's love reaches to the rich and the poor. God's love reaches to the imprisoned and the free. God's love reaches to Muslims, Jews, Hindus, Buddhists and Christians. It reaches to the east and the west, the north and the south. God's love is limitless.

The love of God *reaches to the highest mountain, and flows through the lowest valley. God's love gives us strength... from day to day, and it will never lose its power.*

    God's is a limitless love. It casts out fear... removes doubt... expunges hatred... heals bodies... makes ways out of no way... saves and delivers... it redeems and lifts.

Love divine, all loves excelling
Joy of Heav'n to earth come down
Fix in us thy humble dwelling
All thy faithful mercies crown!
Jesus, Thou art all compassion
Pure unbounded love Thou art
Visit us with Thy salvation
Enter every trembling heart.
(Charles Wesley)

11 - GOD KNOWS

You have searched me, LORD, and you know me. You know when I sit and when I rise; you perceive my thoughts from afar. You discern my going out and my lying down; you are familiar with all my ways. Before a word is on my tongue you, LORD, know it completely. You hem me in behind and before, and you lay your hand upon me. Such knowledge is too wonderful for me, too lofty for me to attain. Where can I go from your Spirit? Where can I flee from your presence? If I go up to the heavens, you are there; if I make my bed in the depths, you are there. If I rise on the wings of the dawn, if I settle on the far side of the sea, even there your hand will guide me, your right hand will hold me fast. (Psalm 139:1-10)

An integral question that lingers within the context of human prayer – our relationality and conversation with God – is what is the nature of God's knowledge of the human predicament. What does God really know about what we are going through? And if God knows, then what does God desire – what does God will – to do about what we perceive to be our needs before God?

A study of scripture shows us that since the beginning of time, God has demonstrated that God knows what we as humans are experiencing. God created the universe, and as a part of creation, God created humanity out of the depths of divine knowledge. God, who created everything, knows everything about that which God created. This is the very nature of God's omniscience.

God's omniscience simply means that God knows everything, about everything, everywhere, and at all times. Furthermore, God's omniscience means that God not only knows what is happening in the present, but God knows what will happen before it happens. We are told by the apostle Paul that God foreknew the coming of Jesus Christ into the world (Romans 8:29). In other words, God knew that Jesus, God's Son, would come into the world even before Jesus was born as the incarnate Son of God, over 2000 years ago.

This is also to say that God's knowledge is different, far more multi-dimensional and vast than what we experience as human knowledge. It has been discovered that human beings only remember (retain) about 10 percent of what we hear and see. That is why I would need to preach this same sermon, to the same people, at least 10 times for us to really get it.

God's knowledge is far more comprehensive than ours. God's knowledge is not merely mental and intellectual – as we have come to perceive human knowledge. God knows us is in an intimate, integral, experiential way. God knows us in a spiritual way.

That God knows us means that God is integrally involved and concerned with every aspect (every nook and cranny) of our lives. It means that God's holiness is connected with the entirety of the human experience. It means that God in God's divine knowledge is concerned with the entirety of the human soul – our mind, emotions and will. God understands how and what we think – how and what we feel – and how and what we desire. That God knows us means that God's holiness connects with our humanity.

The nature of God's knowledge – God's omnipresence – is what the psalmist was writing about in Psalm 139. The psalmist said: *"O Lord, you have searched me and known me. You know my sitting down, and my rising up. You understand my thoughts from afar"* (Psalm 139:1).

What an affirmation of faith from the psalmist that God had searched him and known him. The psalmist could attest to the experiences of many of us. If you are like me, you've been through some times when it seems like there's nobody who understands our particular predicament.

Have you ever been there?

- Nobody understands the sickness that we're experiencing.
- Nobody understands the bills that we have.
- Nobody understands our problems on the job.
- Nobody understands the difficulties we're having with a loved one.

The song-writer put it this way in an old Negro spiritual:

> *Nobody knows the trouble I've seen*
> *Nobody knows my sorrow.*
> *Nobody knows the trouble I've seen*
> *Glory Hallelujah...*

Nobody seems to know – nobody seems to understand – and if they do know and understand, they don't seem to care about what we're going through. *Nobody knows the trouble I've seen...*

But it's good to know that in the midst of it all, God knows. We need to be reminded of this because the trials and tribulations of life are real and inevitable. Disappointment and discouragement are real. We can be on top of the world today, and down in the dumps tomorrow. We can think we know all there is to know, have it all together, and then realize that we find ourselves in the predicament that the great writer James Baldwin wrote about several years ago... *"nobody knows my name..."*

Yes, the reality is that - regardless of who we think we are – regardless of how successful we've become – regardless of how important somebody has made us feel – we all live on the brink of "nobodyness". We all live on the edge of obscurity, insignificance and irrelevance because we can never do enough to please everybody. Indeed, Baldwin's sentiment might ring true for some of us; *"nobody knows my name."*

- I thought I was somebody, but nobody knows my name.
- I have a college degree, but nobody knows my name.
- I've got a good job, but nobody knows my name.
- I've got investments and a retirement account, but nobody knows my name.
- I drive a fine car and live in a nice home, but nobody knows my name.

With all that the psalmist had gone through, what he was really trying to tell his faith community, what he was really trying to affirm, is that God knew all that he had gone through. *"Lord, you have searched me, and you know me."*

Indeed, this is important, because there will be times in all of our lives when there seems to be nobody who cares. The psalmist had to remind himself that:

- Before anybody knew his name – *it was God who had covered him in his mother's womb.*
- Before anybody knew his name - *it was God who had fearfully and wonderfully made him.*
- Before anybody knew his name - *it was God who knew of his substance.*

It's good to know that God knows. In the midst of our "nobodyness", we are all somebody in the sight of God.

Indeed, God knows. Yes, the song-writer said that *"nobody knows the trouble I've seen."* But, it's good to be reminded that that another song-writer came along and wrote about the ways of God in Christ:

There's not a friend like the lowly Jesus.
No, not one. No, not one.
There's not a moment that he does not hear us.
No, not one. No, not one.

Jesus knows all about my struggles
He won't rest until the day is done
There's not a friend like the lowly Jesus
No not one, No not one.
(Johnson Oatman)

12 - IT'S A FAMILY AFFAIR

How very good and pleasant it is when kindred live together in unity! It is like the precious oil on the head, running down upon the beard, on the beard of Aaron, running down over the collar of his robes. It is like the dew of Hermon, which falls on the mountains of Zion. For there the Lord ordained God's blessing, life for evermore. (Psalm 133:1-3)

Music is indeed the soundtrack for many of our lives. We can remember a lot about what was going on in our lives, and in the world, at any given point in time in the past, by the songs we were listening to.

In 1971, the soul band Sly and the Family Stone recorded a song titled "Family Affair".

The lyrics were apropos for the times:

It's a family affair, it's a family affair
It's a family affair, it's a family affair.

One child grows up to be
Somebody that just loves to learn
And another child grows up to be
Somebody you'd just love to burn.

Mom loves the both of them
You see it's in the blood
Both kids are good to Mom
Blood's thicker than mud.

It's a family affair...

The lyrics spoke to some of what was going on in that time – with social upheaval across much of America and the world – and with social and relational turmoil in some families.

"Blood's thicker than mud... It's a family affair." Even with the good and bad, the ups and downs of being family, it's a family affair. The song points to the fact that even in a family, everybody is different and yet – in this case – a mother's love is the glue that holds the family together. *"Blood's thicker than mud."*

The psalmist declared in the Psalm 133:1, *"How very good and pleasant it is for kindred to dwell together in unity"*. It's very good for family, related people, sisters and brothers to live together, and not just live together, but live together in unity.

Psalm 133 has been identified as a form of psalmic literature called Songs of Ascent. These songs – Psalms 120-134 - were most likely sung by Jewish persons as they made their way to Jerusalem – and ascended up to the temple mount to celebrate particular religious festivals like Passover, the Feast of Weeks, and the Feast of Tabernacles.

Persons of Jewish faith would sing these Songs of Ascent as they journeyed. They would sing as means of encouragement and affirmation of who they were and what they were supposed to do as religious people, and most importantly as affirmation of who God was in their lives.

Many of these 15 Songs of Ascent are familiar to us today, like Psalm 121:1, *"I looked to the hills from when cometh my help? My help comes from the Lord,"*, or Psalm 122:1, *"I was glad when they said to me, let us go into the house of the Lord"*, or Psalm 124:1, *"If it had not been for the Lord who was on our side, (where would we be)?"*

And here in Psalm 133, these three short verses begin with the familiar words, *"How very good and pleasant it is for sisters and brothers to dwell together in unity."*

This leads us to first wonder why they would sing a song like this 2900 years ago. Why would they have a need to sing about unity in the context of family back then?

Maybe, things were not much different than as they are now. Maybe then, as now, family structures and cohesion were being challenged. Maybe then, as now, too many children were forced to live in unhealthy and unsafe environments. Maybe then, as now, too many children were growing up with one or both parents being virtually absent from the home.

Maybe, the psalmist needed to sing about unity among kindred because there were people in the religious community and in society at large who couldn't get their minds around what it meant to live with civility, and what harmony, peace and unity should really look like among God's people. Maybe then, as now, there was communal discord, distrust, disengagement, disassociation, dissonance and disintegration.

So, the psalmist needed to remind God's people as they made their way to worship 2900 years ago, *"how very good and pleasant it is for sisters and brother to dwell together in unity.* They needed to sing and remind themselves then, as we do today, that *it's a family affair.*

So, what might we glean from the psalmist's words that can help us in our life together, today?

First, we can glean that unity does not necessarily mean uniformity. Unity means that we learn to dwell together in and across our differences. The uniformity that we have is found in that we have all been created in God's image. But in that uniformity, God has fearfully, uniquely and wonderfully created each of us in particular ways.

Unity then means that in our differences we must learn to dwell together. It means that we must learn how to hang out with some people who stretch us – persons who may not sing like us, pray like us, preach like us, hang out where we normally hang out, or eat the food we like to eat. Unity does not necessarily mean uniformity. Rev. Dr. Martin Luther King, Jr. intimated that "we need to learn to live together was sisters and brothers, or we will perish as fools."

Second, we learn from this psalm that it pleases God when we dwell together in unity – in our homes, in our communities, in our cities, states, nations, and even in our places of worship. The psalmist said, *"How very good and pleasant it is for kindred to dwell together in unity."* In other words, discord doesn't please God, but unity does. Division doesn't please God, but unity pleases God.

Third, God blesses us in our unity. In verse three, the psalmist said, *"For there (in unity) the Lord ordained God's blessing, life forevermore"* (Psalm 133:3).

It's a family affair. God desires and is pleased when we dwell together in unity.

The song-writer, Hezekiah Walker helps us with his song "I Need You to Survive":

I need you; you need me
We're all a part of God's body.
Stand with me, agree with me
We're all a part of God's body.

It is God's will
that every need be supplied.
You are important to me,

61

C. Anthony Hunt
I need you to survive.
(Hezekiah Walker)

13 - WE DON'T DESERVE THIS

God has not dealt with us according to our sins, nor punished us according to our iniquities. As the heavens are high above the earth, so great is God's mercy toward those who fear God. (Psalm 103:10-11)

Sometimes when people ask me how I'm doing, my reply is, "Better than I deserve." I remember a well-meaning person once responding, "Oh no, Tony, you deserve a lot," to which I replied, "Not really." In my responses, I was thinking about what I truly deserve in my human frailty and fallenness — God's judgment. And in light of what I know I really deserve in God's sight, God has been merciful and gracious toward me.

All of us can probably think back over life to times when we received gifts that we did not deserve. There were some material things given to us, or some accolades bestowed on us that we knew that we did not deserve, and that but for the grace of God, the gift would have passed us by.

In psalm 103, the psalmist reminds us that it is time for a reality check when it comes to recognizing some of the ways that God has been at work on our behalf. The psalmist intimated that, *"God has not dealt with us according to our sins, nor punished us according to our iniquities"* (Ps. 103:10).

It appears that those who the psalmist was addressing were a lot like you and me. He knew, and he wanted the people to know that there had been some things that they had done or left undone – some acts of commission or omission - where all they deserved was the wrath – the punishment - of God. There had been some ways that they had treated each other, where they deserved God's judgment. There had been some times when they didn't worship God the way they were supposed to, and what they deserved was God's wrath. And in the midst of God's grace and mercy, they were not recognizing how good and forgiving God had been to them.

One thing we come to realize about sin is that it has a way of hiding itself behind our pride and denial. Either we're too proud to acknowledge the places, spaces and times when we have lived in sin – or we live in such denial that we can't recognize sin in our lives when it's right in our midst. The apostle Paul intimated, *"For I know that good itself does not dwell in me, that is, in my sinful nature. For I have the desire to do what is good, but I cannot carry it out. For I do not do the good I want to do, but the evil I do not want to do-this I keep on doing"* (Romans 7:18-19).

Indeed, it's easy for us to forget how fallen we are at the core of our being, individually and corporately, and how detached we've become – in many ways - from God's will for us. One of the problems with our world today is that too many of us tend to think of ourselves more highly than we should. This diminishes our sense of deep and humble indebtedness to God for God's grace and mercy. It discounts the price that God paid through God's Son, Jesus Christ, to rescue us from our sin.

And so, it helps to take time to consider who we are in light of a holy, just, righteous, merciful and gracious God, and to recognize that the only thing we truly deserve is death. Indeed, Paul said it, *"The wages of sin is death, but the gift of God is eternal life"* (Romans 6:23). Our redemption is an absolute impossibility—except for the gift of Christ's sacrifice on the cross. No wonder the psalmist said, *"As the heavens are high above the earth, so great is God's mercy toward those who fear God"* (Psalm 103:11).

It's good to know that Paul didn't stop by saying that *"the wages of sin is death..."*, but he continued by reminding Christians in Rome, and us today, that *"the gift of God is eternal life"* (Romans 6:23). Justice demanded that we would die, but it's good that God has looked beyond all of our faults, and seen every one of our needs. And so, knowing from how far God as brought us, we can't help but sing, *"Amazing grace, how sweet the sound!"*

When thinking about the gift that God has given us, and what Christ has done in our lives, I remember days past when my grandmother collected S&H Green Stamps for the items she purchased from the grocery store. As she collected green stamps, she would put them in her stamp book. When my grandmother had collected enough green stamps, she would then take the stamp book to the store to exchange it – to redeem the stamps - for a special household item that she had been wanting and waiting to have.

Ultimately, that is what Christ has done for us. Christ came into the world, and has entered into our lives to be our redemption, to buy us back, and claim us for God. Indeed, *"God demonstrated God's love toward us in that while we were yet sinners, Christ died for us"* (Roman 5:8).

God has given us more than we deserve. And so, we ought to thank God for not dealing with us according to our iniquities. If God never does anything more than redeem us, God has already done far more than we deserve.

We need to know and acknowledge that we are indebted to God for the love and grace that God in Christ demonstrated on the cross to purchase our pardon and forgiveness—far beyond what we deserve!

C. Anthony Hunt

Amazing grace! How sweet the sound
That saved a wretch like me!
I once was lost, but now am found;
Was blind, but now I see.

Through many dangers, toils, and snares,
I have already come;
'Tis grace hath brought me safe thus far,
And grace will lead me home.
(John Newton)

14 - ENCOURAGEMENT FOR THE DIRECTIONALLY CHALLENGED
(TURN ON YOUR GPS)

Your Word is a lamp to my feet and a light to my path. (Psalm 119:105 (105-112))
Teach me, LORD, the way of your decrees, that I may follow it to the end. Give me understanding, so that I may keep your law and obey it with all my heart. Direct me in the path of your commands, for there I find delight. Turn my heart toward your statutes and not toward selfish gain. Turn my eyes away from worthless things; preserve my life according to your word. Fulfill your promise to your servant, so that you may be feared. Take away the disgrace I dread, for your laws are good. How I long for your precepts! In your righteousness preserve my life. (Psalm 119:33-40)

A feature on many automobiles today is what is known as a GPS – a Global Positioning System. Long gone – it seems – are the days of using maps, atlases, and MapQuest to help us get to the places we want to go. If the truth is told, many people today would not know what to do if we did not have some type of GPS to help us navigate from place to place. Many people would be lost today if we had to depend on our ability to read a map to get to where we wanted to go.

One important feature of the GPS is the "reset" or "redirection" feature – where the GPS will automatically, or at the push of a button, reset or redirect us if we make a wrong turn, miss a turn, or in some other way get off the prescribed course, and find ourselves on the verge of getting lost. A characteristic of the GPS is that if it is really up-to-date, and is really doing its job, it will get us to where we want to go, the fastest way, with the least amount of traffic, along the way.

A problem lies in that many of us sometimes think we're smarter than the GPS, and we decide that we're going to take a turn that is not prescribed, and then we get off course and may end up getting lost. The Global Positioning System will then remind us that we're off course by saying, "Your route is now being redirected."

In Psalm 119, the psalmist was also in need of direction, and perhaps some redirection. So, he had enough sense to go to God and ask for help. Here, the psalmist asked God for seven things: *(1) to teach him God's ways, (2) to give him understanding, (3) to direct him in God's paths where he could find delight, (4) to turn his heart toward God's teachings, (5) to turn his eyes away from worthless things and preserve his life, (6) to fulfill God's promises in his life, and (7) to take away any disgrace in his life.*

The psalmist was directionally challenged. He realized how needy he was, and went to God and prayed for the seven specific things that he needed God to do to turn his life around, and put him on the right path. He was praying for a different kind of GPS, *God's Protection System,* that God would protect him, provide for him, and position him to walk and live in the ways of the Lord.

A reminder for us today is that we are likewise in some ways needy, in need of *God's Protection System* in our lives. The season of Lent is one of repentance and redirection. In the forty days, plus six Sundays of Lent, we have the opportunity to turn back to God – make a right turn or U-turn back to God and place ourselves more fully in the will, and at the disposal of God.

Maybe it was a "Lenten season" for the psalmist, and maybe he realized how important it was for him to seize the opportunity to call on the name of the Lord, turn around, turn back, and make a right-turn or U-turn back to God.

So it is with our spiritual lives. So often people try to make it through life without God's direction and light. If the truth is told, many of us have been there.

We've tried to wade through the troubled waters of life on our own – without God in our lives. We've tried to get by on our intellect, our talent, our possessions, even our appearance – only to reach the point where we realize that without God, we don't really know where we are going – having no real direction and no light – lost and blind.

In Psalm 119, the psalmist offered a remedy for the directionally challenged among us. Based on his own experience with God, he talked to God and reminded God of something that God already knows, *"Your Word is a lamp to my feet and a light to my path"* (Psalm 119:105).

God's Word is like a GPS in uncertain times. It is full of the promises we need to keep us from driving our lives into the ditch of bitterness and despair, disappointment, discouragement, and lostness.

Maybe the psalmist realized that he was like a lot of people who Paul would talk to about 900 years later, and remind them that *"all have sinned and come short of the glory of God"* (Romans 3:23). Maybe the psalmist had come to the realization in an existential way that *"the wages of sin is death, but the gift of God is eternal life"* (Romans 6:23). Maybe he could anticipate what Solomon would preach near that time that this psalm was written, that *"if my people who are called by my name would humble themselves and pray, and turn from their wicked ways, (God said) I will hear their prayers and heal the land"* (2 Chronicles 7:14).

Maybe the psalmist could anticipate that we'd need a word about the need in this present day to turn on our GPS – *God's Protection System.*

With all that confronts us individually and collectively today – ups and downs, joys and pains, sunshine and rain, trials and tribulations, valleys and vicissitudes, uncertainty and worry, sickness, death, religious disunity, social distress and political discord – the psalmist's words are a reminder to us that we need turn on our GPS.

The psalmist's words are a reminder that God is a present help in all of our times of trouble. They are a reminder that God is an on-time, all the time, every time, any time God. Whatever we need today, God has it.

God still specializes in looking beyond all of our faults, and seeing all of our needs.

So, let's be determined to turn on our GPS.

The next time you feel as if you're walking in the dark, remember to trust your GPS —*God's Protection System.*

Indeed, the Word of God is a lamp and light for us. We need to see the way, and God's Word shows us what we need to know so that we won't go astray.

God's Word promises that *"God will never leave us nor forsake us"* (Heb. 13:5). God's Word assures us that *"God knows the plans God has for us, plans for our wholeness and not for harm, to give us a future and a hope"* (Jer. 29:11).

If we put our trust in God and God's Word, and walk in God's light, God won't let us stumble, fall or lose our way.

Be not dismayed, whatever betide

God will take care of you.
Beneath God's wings of love abide
God will take care of you.

God will take care of you
Through everyday o'er all the way.
God will care for you
God will take care of you.
(Civilla Durfee Martin)

15 - WHEN PEACE IS POSSIBLE

I was glad when they said to me, "Let us go to the house of the LORD!" Our feet are standing within your gates, O Jerusalem. Jerusalem built as a city that is bound firmly together. To it the tribes go up, the tribes of the LORD, as was decreed for Israel, to give thanks to the name of the LORD. For there the thrones for judgment were set up, the thrones of the house of David. Pray for the peace of Jerusalem: "May they prosper who love you. Peace be within your walls, and security within your towers." For the sake of my relatives and friends I will say, "Peace be within you." For the sake of the house of the LORD our God, I will seek your good. (Psalm 122:1-9)

In Psalm 122, we find ourselves at what is known in psalmic literature as a Song of Ascent. The Hebrew word *"ma – lah"* means ascent, step-up, or rising. It means to go up, to strive toward a higher place.

The backdrop of Psalm 122, this Song of Ascent is that it is one of 15 similar songs (Psalms 120-134) that comprise a long-playing album of songs of aspiring and ascent. In common artistic vernacular, these 15 Songs of Ascent, are a mix-tape – an extended play (EP) album - on how God's people, Israel, aspired to see God, and know more fully the ways of the Lord.

We recall that in Psalm 121, the psalmist had sung in that Song of Ascent, *"I looked to the hills, from whence comes my help? My help comes from the Lord"* (Psalm 121:1). The people of God were striving to get to a higher place – higher ground - and here is implied the hardships, dangers, toils and snares involved in their upward journey. And here, it is further implied that Israel knew that only with the Lord's help would they make it to where they wanted to be.

In Psalm 121:1, David ended by declaring that, *"My help comes from the Lord."* Some of us can attest to how difficult the journey of life can be and we can testify, like David, that we know that indeed *"our help comes from the Lord."* We can testify also that *"if it had not been for the Lord who was on our side, the Lord only knows where we would be"* (Psalm 124:1). We can declare that as we have climbed up the rough side of life's mountains, it has been God's grace and mercy that have abided with us, and carried us along the way.

And we can look back and thank God even for the rough places on the sides of the mountains we've had to climb, for as it has been intimated by others, without the rough places on the sides of mountains – if the sides of mountains had been all smooth - we might not have been able to climb to the top, and get to where God intended for us to be. God helps us to climb to higher ground.

This higher ground is what soul singer, Stevie Wonder alluded to in his song:
I'm so darn glad He let me try it again
'Cause my last time on earth I lived a whole world of sin
I'm so glad that I know more than I knew then
Gonna keep on tryin'
'Til I reach my highest ground.
(Higher Ground)

And now, as we make our way to Psalm 122, the third song in this holy and divine mix-tape, David begins with the familiar words and tag to this song, *"I was glad when they said to me, let us go into the house of the Lord."* After all of their journeying, sweating and struggling, tears and toil, after all of their wanting to give up and turn around, after all of their tired feet and weary souls - the people of God had made it to God's house, made it into the presence of the Lord, and David could then declare that *"I was glad when they said to me, let us go into the house of the Lord."*

But an inherent challenge with this text is that many people stop at this first verse, *"I was glad when they said to me..."* If we are to listen down into the song, and hear a little more of the lyrics, we hear what's really at stake. *Peace.*

Beginning in verse 6, David began to let the people of God know what was really at stake when they made their way into God's presence – *peace.* Let's listen in. David said in verses 6-8:

> *Pray for the peace of Jerusalem: "May they prosper who love you. Peace be within your walls, and security within your towers." For the sake of my relatives and friends I will say, "Peace be within you."*

As we make our way to the end of 2020, it seems that we find ourselves at a similar place as the people of Israel found themselves about 2900 years ago. Today, we face the pandemic of violence where over 300 of God's people have been killed in Baltimore for the sixth consecutive year. We face the pandemics of racism – where we are left to wonder whether Black Lives really do matter in America. We face the pandemic of COVID-19 that has wrecked all of our reality in 2020, where now millions of people have died around the world. We face the pandemic of economic despair which has left millions of people around the world at points of joblessness, food and housing insecurity.

And like David proclaimed to the people of Israel that they were to pray for the peace of Jerusalem, and that just as importantly pray that peace would be within them, we are likewise encouraged, amidst pandemic and pandemonium, to pray for peace.

The story of Christ is really the story of peace. The Church's story is that of the Prince of Peace, Jesus who came into the world to give us peace. The apostle Paul proclaimed that *"Christ is our peace who has destroyed the walls of hostility"* (Ephesians 2:14).

This peace is an eternal gift from God to the world. Christ is the Prince of Peace. He is our peace. God's presence in Christ is not episodic, it is not temporary or conditional; God's peace in Christ is ever-present, eternal and everlasting.

And so, just as David encouraged the people of his day as they made their way into God's house, might it be so that God will grant each of us peace, and might it be so that God would rain peace in the world.

God's promise to us is that God will keep us in *"perfect peace (as our) minds are stayed on God"* (Isaiah 26:3). God will give us *"peace that passes all understanding"* (Philippians 4:7).

Lord, make us instruments of your peace.
Where there is hatred, let us sow love;
where there is injury, pardon;
where there is doubt, faith;
where there is despair, hope;
where there is darkness, light;
where there is sadness, joy.
(St. Francis of Assisi)

16 - WHEN GOD WORKS

How many are your works, Lord! In wisdom you made them all; the earth is full of your creatures. There is the sea, vast and spacious, teeming with creatures beyond number— living things both large and small. There the ships go to and fro, and Leviathan, which you formed to frolic there. All creatures look to you to give them their food at the proper time. When you give it to them, they gather it up; when you open your hand, they are satisfied with good things. When you hide your face, they are terrified; when you take away their breath, they die and return to the dust. When you send your Spirit, they are created, and you renew the face of the ground. (Psalm 104:24-30)

When the day of Pentecost came, they were all together in one place. Suddenly a sound like the blowing of a violent wind came from heaven and filled the whole house where they were sitting. They saw what seemed to be tongues of fire that separated and came to rest on each of them. All of them were filled with the Holy Spirit and began to speak in other tongues as the Spirit enabled them. (Acts 2:1-4)

The psalmist's concern in Psalm 104 is with extolling God because of God's manifold, magnificent works. The concern here is with how God has been present and evident in creation; how God has been at work in creation. *"How many are your works, Lord! In wisdom you made them all; the earth is full of your creatures"* (Psalm 104:24).

If there is anything that the world needs today, it is that we need to acknowledge that God has been at work, that God continues to be at work, and that God will continue to work in the days ahead, and through eternity.

There is much today that could lead some of us to doubt the power, presence and provision of God. With all of the turmoil and tumult that exists in the world, with all of the trials and tribulations swirling around us, some might wonder, "where in the world is God?"

Indeed, if there is anything that we need today, it is the belief and confidence in knowing that God is real, God is at work, and that we can depend on God. Others may be dependable, but when all is said and done, it's good to know that God is forever, and everywhere dependable. God is not dead, God is not done, nor is God inactive, but God is alive, well and working.

God has been, and is, real, and is working in and for us. God's spirit breathed into nothing and created heaven and earth. God breathed into Adam and Eve, and humanity came to be. God breathed into Godself, and sent God's only begotten Son and our Savior, Jesus Christ, into the world about 2000 years ago. And God breathed new life, fresh wind and fire, on the day of Pentecost, and the Church came into being. God specializes in creating things. God specializes in breathing life into the world. Indeed, God has been, and continues to be alive, well and working in all creation.

This is what the psalmist was celebrating in Psalm 104. He was giving the Lord thanks and praise for what the Lord has created, the work that God has done.

And the truth of the matter is that if we do some assessment of our lives today, the psalmist would not be alone in his estimation of God's work. If we take time to stop and count our blessings, we will find ourselves at a similar place as the psalmist, joining him in praising God for what the Lord has done for us, God's work in our lives.

God has worked in every one of our lives, in particular ways. And if we just paused and took a praise break, we could declare just like the psalmist in Psalm 104:24, *"Lord, how many are your works!"*

That is the real story of Pentecost. Pentecost is not just a history lesson about how the Holy Spirit moved 2000 years ago, but it is an affirmation of how the Spirit of the living God is moving, being and working in and through us right now.

You name it, and God has done it. The Spirt of the living God has been, and continues to be at work in the world. God woke us up today, and started us on our way. God put blood in our veins, activity in our limbs, walking and running in our feet, speech on our lips, thoughts in our minds, clothes on our backs, food on our tables, and shelter over our heads.

And in Psalm 104, the psalmist teaches us one important lesson about the work that God does in our lives. And that lesson is that when God breathes, when God works, when God blesses in manifold and magnificent ways, there is really only one appropriate response for us. That response is to praise God for what the Lord has done.

The psalmist praised God for all that the Lord had created, the great work that God had done in his life, the life of God's people and all of creation.

What mighty works might we take time to praise God for today? How might we extol and magnify the Lord for the great things God has done in our lives? Might our life's doxology be:

Praise God from whom all blessings flow.
Praise God, all creatures here below.

Praise God above the heavenly host.
Praise Father, Son, and Holy Ghost!

17 – OBEY YOUR THIRST

As the deer pants for streams of water, so my soul pants for you, my God. My soul thirsts for God, for the living God. When can I go and meet with God? My tears have been my food day and night, while people say to me all day long, "Where is your God?" **(Psalm 42:1-3)**

Growing up, our paternal grandparents lived across the road from a well. I can remember playing outside on hot summer days, and there would come points when we knew that it was time to stop playing, for we were thirsty. And it was time for us to go to the well.

We would go to the well, and pump it until water came flowing out. We'd pump and pump, and there was nothing like the sight of seeing water finally begin to gush out of the well, and nothing like knowing that our thirst would then be quenched.

I would venture to suggest that all of us have found ourselves at points of being thirsty from time to time. Being thirsty places us at the point of needing to address one of the basic necessities of life. The fact is that we can't survive without water.

Without water, we'd eventually find ourselves at the point of being dehydrated, and we would eventually die. To be thirsty is to experience the most basic and profound of human needs. It has been suggested that thirst is such a powerful longing that it displaces all other desires.

In the scripture text, we find that the writer of Psalm 42 was obviously yearning for a closer relationship with God. He was seeking and searching for something more, something deeper in his spiritual walk and relationship with God.

And so, the psalmist began his song with a metaphor of a thirsty, panting deer. Let's listen in on the psalmist: *"As the deer pants for streams of water, so my soul pants for you, my God. My soul thirsts for God, for the living God. When can I go and meet with God?" (Psalm 42:1-2)*

The image here is of a deer that is frantically panting and searching in the desert for a stream of water to quench its thirst, and satisfy its physical need.

Though the psalmist pointed to the panting deer's longing in the midst of physical thirst, desire and danger - this metaphor offers a profound spiritual image and reminder for us that our relationship with God is as essential to our spiritual well-being as water is to our physical well-being.

With the same passion and intensity as the panting deer seeks water, the psalmist was seeking after God. He was speaking to a need that is common among all of us. An integral part of the human plight is our need to know and to experience God.

This is what St. Augustine of Hippo spoke of in his prayer, *"Lord, you have created us for yourself, and our souls are restless until they find their rest in you."*

This message is for some of us who find ourselves at the place where our souls are likewise restless for God. This is a word for those who are seriously searching and seeking a closer relationship and walk with the Lord. This is encouragement for those who are like the panting deer, and we are thirsty for God.

And the encouragement for us it to *obey your thirst.*

"As the deer pants for streams of water, so my soul pants for you, my God."

In this contemporary and commercial age, many forms of beverage have emerged that claim to be thirst-quenchers. Just go into the grocery store and we will find on the shelves any number of so-called thirst-quenching products. There's Smart Water, flavored water, vitamin water, Gatorade, Powerade, and any number of other products. But, there's still something that leads me to believe that none of these thirst-quenchers really take the place of water itself.

We've now fully bought into the bottled water explosion. It is now a multi-billion-dollar, global phenomenon. Look on store shelves, and we find that there are any number of brands of bottled water - all claiming to offer something different than the next brand.

Some brands claim to be purer than others. Others claim to have fewer chemicals, some claim to have more natural minerals, and others claim to come from regions of the world where the environment is not as polluted as others.

Still, there's one fundamental claim that all of these brands of bottled water hold to. It's that they will quench our thirst.

And while all these products may quench our physical thirst for a moment, we'll get thirsty again. And furthermore, these products might quench our physical thirst, but we all long for something more, something deeper in life.

What are you really thirsty for today? What are the things that you most desire in life? What are your heart's desires? What are the things that you seek after? How are you seeking after God? The psalmist declared, *"My soul thirsts for God, for the living God."*

The encouragement is to obey your thirst. *It's good to know Jesus. And it's good to know that Jesus is our living water. And when we walk with Jesus, we walk with a well of life that will never run dry.* Jesus said, *"Everyone who drinks the water I will give them will never be thirsty again"* (John 4:14).

When we were young, and got thirsty, we knew when it was time to stop and go to the well, and get refreshed, renewed and regenerated. We knew when it was time to stop and obey our thirst.

Let's likewise be encouraged today to obey our thirst. Let's be encouraged to go to the well. Let's be encouraged to seek and search after the living water. Let's be encouraged to seek and search after Jesus, and he will give us *flowing, refreshing, renewing, regenerating water – and we will thirst no more.*

18 - I PUT IT ALL IN GOD'S HANDS

In you, Lord, I have taken refuge; let me never be put to shame; deliver me in your righteousness. Turn your ear to me, come quickly to my rescue; be my rock of refuge, a strong fortress to save me. Since you are my rock and my fortress, for the sake of your name lead and guide me. Keep me free from the trap that is set for me, for you are my refuge. Into your hands I commit my spirit; deliver me, Lord, my faithful God. (Psalm 31:1-5)

One of the most memorable and meaningful songs of my growing up is one with which I'm sure many of us are familiar –

God's got the whole world in God's hands...
God's got the whole world in God's hands...
God's got you and me sister in God's hands...
God's got you and me brother in God's hands...
God's got the little bitty children in God's hands...
God's got the whole world in God's hands.

What a marvelous proclamation and affirmation of faith - that God has the whole world God's hands. Over 2900 years ago, David came to the point of a similar affirmation in his life.

In Psalm 31, David used the first five verses to render a prayer to God. His was a prayer of reflection and petition, as he looked back over his life, and reflected on some of the things that he had gone through, and some of the things that could have taken him out.

David prayed to God about very particular things in his life – *(1) that God would not let him be put to shame, (2) that God would rescue him, (3) that God would be his protection, (4) that God would deliver him, (5) that God would lead and guide him, and (6) that God would keep him from falling into traps that had been set for him.* David reflected on the fact that God had been his refuge, rock and fortress in the past, and he prayed that God would be so in the future. *"In you Lord, I have taken refuge"* (v. 1).

That David prayed for the specific things that he needed God to do for him should be instructive for us in that we should likewise be about the business of praying for the particular things we need God to be and do in our lives. Our prayer lives should be modeled after David's.

If we need healing, we should pray for healing. If we need deliverance, we should pray for deliverance. If we need provision, we should pray for provision. If we need protection, we should pray for protection. If we need peace of mind and spirit, we should pray for peace.

We pray to God for what we need because God is a prayer-answering God, and God inclines God's ears to hear our prayers, and answers our prayers according the specific things we ask for and the specific things we need in our lives.

Then David concluded by telling God *"Into your hands I commit my spirit; deliver me, Lord, my faithful God"* (v. 5).

It is interesting that the final words of David's prayer in Psalm 31 are the last words that Jesus spoke from the cross at his crucifixion. According to Luke, *"Then Jesus, crying with a loud voice, said, 'Father, into your hands I commend my spirit.' Having said this, he breathed his last"* (Luke 23:46).

David and Jesus had enough sense to put their spirits in God's hands. Later in Psalm 31, David again addressed God, entrusting his life to the Lord, *"My times are in your hand"* (v. 15). David put his life in the hand of the Lord. He had faith to believe that he could commend his life, his spirit, into God's hands.

The image of God's hand is powerful because a hand is that which holds and handles. A hand carries. A hand manages. A hand keeps us when we need to be kept. A hand helps us when we need to be helped.

David had faith to put his life in God's hands because he knew that God could and would hold him and handle any and every situation that would come his way.

When we put our lives in God's hands, we're in good hands. And we're in good hands because we're in God's hands. We know that the All-State Insurance company commercializes that we're in good hands when we buy their insurance, but it's good to know that we're in the best hands when we're in the Lord's hands.

It's good to know that we can put our lives in God's hands, and it's good to know that we're in good hands when we're in God's hands. Indeed, of all the things that God's hands do, *God's hands hold and they handle.*

It's good to know that God will hold us in the cup of God's divine hands. God holds us and rocks us as a parent rocks a child. God holds us in God's care, and won't let anything or anybody mess with God's own.

And God's hands not only hold, but God's hands handle. The great news is that God will handle whatever comes our way in life:

- If we're sick, God will handle it.
- If we're broke, God will handle it.

- If we're broken, God will handle it.
- If we're sad, God will handle it.
- If we're mad, God will handle it.

Whatever we need, and wherever we find ourselves on life's journey, we're in good hands.

Why? Because we're in God's hands.

Indeed, we're in good hands, because we're in God's hands.

We are encouraged to put our lives in God's hands because with whatever we are going through, we can rest assured that God can and will handle whatever it is in our lives that needs to be handled.

Death and distress - God will handle it. Disappointment, discouragement and despair - God will handle it. Trials, tribulations, troubles, tumult, valleys, virulence, vicissitudes - God will handle it. Ups and downs, joys and pain, sunshine and rain - God will handle it.

Whatever we need God to handle, God can, and will handle it. Healing for our bodies, God will handle it. Deliverance in despair, God will handle it. Salvation for our souls, God will handle it.

We may try to fix things ourselves, figure things out, and work things out on our own, but we will come to the same conclusion as David, and *put it all in God's hands.*

When we look up, God shows up. When we get out of the way, God has God's way.

I put it all in God's hands.

C. Anthony Hunt

Time is filled with swift transition.
Naught of earth unmoved can stand.
Build your hopes on things eternal.
Hold to God's unchanging hand.
(Jennie Wilson)

19 - STRENGTH IN A STORM

God is our refuge and strength, a very present help in trouble. Therefore, we will not fear, though the earth should change, though the mountains shake in the heart of the sea; though its waters roar and foam, though the mountains tremble with its tumult. (Psalm 46:1-3)

Immediately, Jesus made the disciples get into the boat and go on ahead of him to the other side, while he dismissed the crowd. After he had dismissed them, he went up on a mountainside by himself to pray. Later that night, he was there alone, and the boat was already a considerable distance from land, buffeted by the waves because the wind was against it. Shortly before dawn Jesus went out to them, walking on the lake. When the disciples saw him walking on the lake, they were terrified. "It's a ghost," they said, and cried out in fear. But Jesus immediately said to them: "Take courage! It is I. Don't be afraid." (Matthew 14:22-27)

In these past several weeks, with the reality of COVID-19, coronavirus, now with us, we are reminded of the fragility of life. Life is fragile. We are aware, perhaps more than ever, of a few things - that life really matters, that all life is important, that every day is a day to cherish, that every blessing is a point of thanksgiving, that tomorrow is not promised, and that relationships and community are gifts from God.

Indeed, tragedy and suffering have a way of shedding light on the things that really matter. Even before the full extent of the devastation is known, we are stunned into silence when we experience the power of forces that are, in many ways, out of our control, and that stand to threaten and destroy our sense of normalcy, security, comfort and peace. When the way we have known the world to be, the way life and health have been, are in some ways swept away like a hundred mile-an-hour wind, we are left to reflect on the meaning of it all, and the meaning of life itself.

But even in times like these, assurance can be found in and through our faith in God. Hear the psalmist in the midst of his own trials and travails – *"God is our refuge and strength, a very present help in trouble"* (Psalm 46:1).

We can testify to the fact that troubles, trials, tribulations, travail and tumult will come, but we live with the blessed assurance, in the midst of whatever difficulties may come, that God is and always will be *our refuge and strength, a very present help in trouble.*

Let's hear the psalmist again:

> *Therefore, we will not fear, though the earth should change, though the mountains shake in the heart of the sea; though its waters roar and foam, though the mountains tremble with its tumult"* (v. 2-3).

We've learned lately, as the hymn intimates, that *"Life is indeed filled with swift transition"*. Yet, in the midst of whatever we are facing, with faith in God, we need not fear; again, we are reminded *"though the mountains shake in the heart of the sea; though its waters roar and foam, though the mountains tremble with its tumult" (v. 3)* – we need not be afraid, for God is the author and finisher of all that is and is to be.

Indeed, one of the evidentiary purposes of God, in sending God's only begotten Son, Jesus, to earth, was to show the world some things. God decided to wrap Godself in human flesh some 2000 years ago, show up as God incarnate, and demonstrate during Jesus's earthly life and ministry that we are never outside the presence of God.

We are never alone. Jesus had another name from his more ancient Hebrew heritage - *Immanuel - God is with us.*

This is something that Peter was reminded of one day on a stormy sea. He, needed a memory lesson about who Jesus really is. Peter's experience should resonate with some of what we are experiencing amidst the pandemic storm realities that are ours to live today.

One night, Peter and the other disciples were sailing across the Sea of Galilee when a strong storm arose. All of a sudden, Jesus showed up walking on water. Naturally, this took the disciples by surprise. *He reassured them: "Take courage! It is I. Don't be afraid"* (Matthew 14:27).

Peter impulsively asked Jesus if he could join Him. He stepped out of the boat and walked toward Jesus. But Peter soon lost focus, became aware of the dangerous and humanly impossible situation he was in, and started sinking.

He cried out, *"Lord, save me!"* and Jesus lovingly reached out his hand, caught Peter, and rescued him (Matthew 14:30–31).

Many of us may have felt like Peter lately; felt as though we're sinking amidst the storms that we're in, and furthermore felt as though we're sinking while trying to walk on the turbulent waters of life.

Indeed, many of us can relate to Peter because we've been on similar seas lately - crying out to the Lord to help and rescue us while we feel like we are sinking - with the pandemic experiences of isolation, crying out of concerns for our own health and that of loved ones, crying out of worry about financial difficulties, crying out of uncertainty about what the future holds.

The prevailing sentiment of Peter and his fellow disciples was fear. They were frightened... afraid... fearful... scared.

And some of us might say that to be afraid is to be unfaithful. But I'd like to suggest that to be afraid is to be human. To be afraid is to be true to who we really are. To be afraid is to realize that we are at a point where we can't handle the predicaments that we find ourselves in by ourselves, and that we need God to be our very present help.

If we're honest with ourselves, we will all be afraid from time to time. And for people who walk by faith and not by sight, to be afraid is to be at a place where we realize that only with God's help will we get out of the vicissitudinous predicaments we may be in. To be afraid and to walk by faith is to walk on the waters of life realizing that Jesus walks with us every step of the way. To be afraid and to walk by faith is to know that Jesus will come to see about us amidst the storms that life will bring our way.

What are some lessons of faith that we can glean from Peter's encounter with Jesus on the stormy Sea of Galilee?

First, our faith grants us the assurance that we are not alone. In the midst of Peter's fear, Jesus said to him and the disciples - *"Take courage! It is I. Don't be afraid".* Jesus wanted Peter to know that amidst his fears and uncertainty, he was not alone, and that Jesus would never leave him or forsake him.

Second, our faith grants us the assurance that it's all right to ask a God for help. A faithful act amidst our fears is to ask the Lord for help. Peter cried out as he was sinking - *"Lord, save me!"* Perhaps, our most faithful act in pandemic, tsunamic, stormy seasons of our lives is to cry out, and pray to the Lord as Peter did, *"Lord, save us"*. When is the last time we called on God to be our *"refuge and strength, our very present help"* in the midst of the trouble we are in?

Third, our faith grants us the assurance that Jesus specializes in saving us. *Jesus reached out his hand, caught Peter, and saved him.* Indeed, like Peter, we can be assured that Jesus is with us even in the storms of life! *Jesus is strength our storms.* He speaks to storms and says, *"peace",* and the winds and storms obey him.

Jesus said, *"let not your hearts be troubled"* (John 14:1). Why? Because he is with us. Whatever storms will come upon us, however long the rain of life will last, whatever the strength of the winds that come to buffet us, *we are never alone.* He's strength in our storms.

Thanks be to God who has blessed us with faith that supersedes fear, and faith that will keep us and hold us in times like these.

When the storms of life are raging,
stand by me; (stand by me)
when the storms of life are raging,
stand by me. (stand by me)
When the world is tossing me
like a ship upon the sea,
thou who rulest wind and water,
stand by me. (stand by me).
(Charles Albert Tindley)

20 - WE ARE NOT ALONE

The Lord is close to the brokenhearted, and saves those who are crushed in spirit. *(Psalm 34:18)*

In 1965, soul singer Jimmy Ruffin posed a provocative, searing and penetrating question in a memorable song, *"What Becomes of the Brokenhearted"*.
Ruffin sang –

What becomes of the brokenhearted
Who had love that's now departed?
I know I've got to find
Some kind of peace of mind.
Help me.

Ruffin's predicament of, and question about, being brokenhearted is one with which each and every one of us will be acquainted at some points on life's journey. The truth is that things will happen, trials will come, storms will show up, and situations will arise that will break our hearts. That's life. That's the way of the world.

The psalmist must have been similarly well-acquainted with having been
brokenhearted, and sang about it in Psalm 34 as encouragement for his soul, and encouragement for others, then and now, who would, likewise, experience being broken.

Psalm 34 is identified as a song of David, and is believed to have been written about the events surrounding when David pretended to be insane before Abimelek, who drove him away, and David left. (That event is recorded in 1 Samuel 21:13.) In fleeing from Saul, David sought refuge in the city of Gath—the hometown of the warrior Goliath who

David had killed in battle. When the people of Gath protested David's presence in their city, he pretended to be insane in order to escape.

It may seem that David escaped danger and possible death by his own resourcefulness and skill, but he clearly gives God the glory, credit and appreciation for his escape.

We notice that David's song of encouragement is sung within the context of the people's faith experience. His song is encouragement for religious people, and should be a reminder for each of us who walks by faith and not by sight that we will not be immune to broken-heartedness.

Our faith and faithfulness do not make us immune to disappointments and despair. Disappointment and despair will come, and we will need the same assurance that David offered the saints of his day. *"The Lord is close to the brokenhearted, and saves those who are crushed in spirit"* (Psalm 34:18).

What our faith does in the midst of brokenness is that it inclines us to turn to God in times of crisis to ask the question – "Where is God?" When we are brokenhearted, we may feel that God is far away.

And David's song is also indicative that we are not the first people of faith to have broken hearts, and to have questions as to God's proximity. We find this in other psalms as well. Psalm 10 begins, *"Why, O Lord, do you stand far off? Why do you hide yourself in times of trouble?"* Psalm 13 begins, *"How long, O Lord? Will you forget me forever? How long will you hide your face from me?"* Psalm 22 begins, *"My God, my God, why have you forsaken me? Why are you so far from helping me, from the words of my groaning?"*

Broken-heartedness that is incumbent for all of those who are suffering from COVID-19, all of those have lost loved ones, all of those who have lost jobs and livelihoods, all of those who wonder about their future. And it has come upon those who have faith in God, just as it has upon those who may not have faith.

In 1905, Charles Tindley sang words similar to those of David to people of faith of his day, when he penned these lyrics:

When the storms of life are raging,
Stand by me (stand by me);
When the storms of life are raging,
Stand by me (stand by me);
When the world is tossing me
Like a ship upon the sea,
Thou Who rulest wind and water,
Stand by me (stand by me).

And in 1932, amidst his own broken-heartedness, Thomas Dorsey penned the familiar lyrics:

Precious Lord, take my hand
Lead me on, let me stand.
I'm tired, I'm weak, I'm worn.
Through the storm, through the night
Lead me on to the light.
Take my hand precious Lord, lead me home.

So, what then is the remedy and recourse for broken-heartedness? What becomes of the brokenhearted?

David encouraged the people of his day with these words of assurance – *"The Lord is close to the brokenhearted, and saves those who are crushed in spirit"* (Ps. 34:18).

Perhaps that is why Tindley could pray in his song *"When the storms of life are raging (Lord) stand by me."* Perhaps that is why Dorsey likewise could pray, *"Precious Lord, take my hand.*

Maybe they knew, like David knew, that *the Lord is close to the brokenhearted.* The blessed assurance for us is that in and through any difficulties we face, any trials and tribulations that come our way – we are not alone. *The Lord is close to the brokenhearted. The Lord is close to us. We are not alone.*

Indeed, we can rest assured that God has not changed. The same God who was close David is close to you and me. The same God who was close to Tindley and Dorsey will be close to you and me today and tomorrow. *We are not alone.*

God knows. God understands. God loves. God cares. God heals. God protects. God provides. God saves. And we can rest assured that *"the Lord is always close to the brokenhearted"* (Psalm 34:18). God will come to see about us. Jesus said, *"I will never leave you or forsake you. I will be with you, even until the end of the age"* (Matthew 28:20). *We are not alone.*

I heard the voice of Jesus saying
Come into me and rest.
Lie down thy weary one, lie down
Thy head upon min breast.
I came to Jesus as I was,
I was weary, worn and sad.
And I found in him a resting place,
And he had made he glad!
(Horatius Bonar)

21 - WHAT TRIALS CAN TEACH US

Praise our God, all peoples, let the sound of God's praise be heard; God has preserved our lives and kept our feet from slipping. For you, God, tested us; you refined us like silver. You brought us into prison and laid burdens on our backs. You let people ride over our heads; we went through fire and water, but you brought us to a place of abundance. (Psalm 66:8-12)

Placed in a predicament of having wondered as to the presence of God within the context of their trials, tribulations and trouble, the Israelites had understandably become weary, worn and worried in their faith. How could they praise God and keep the faith in the midst of their difficulties?

This is no easy question for any of us to answer. We will all, at points, find ourselves at the place and predicament of the Israelites. What gives us impetus to offer praise to God, especially on either side of – or in the midst of - going through difficulties, despair and distress?

The Israelites found themselves on the other side of having gone through some trials. Psalm 66 is a song of remembrance and praise about God having saved and delivered God's people from almost certain destruction and annihilation that could have taken them out.

And now they knew that if it had not been for the Lord who was on their side, they didn't know if they would have made it out and over their difficulties.

In a prayer, the psalmist took time to remind God that the people had endured some things. *"For you, God, tested us; you refined us like silver. You brought us into prison and laid burdens on our backs. You let people ride over our heads; we went through fire and water"* (Psalm 66:11-12).

It is important to note that God's will for us is not always experienced within the context of God's *perfect will.* The will of God is sometimes experienced within the context of God's *permissive will.* This can't be fully explained in the human realm, but the record will show that God, in God's *permissive will* sometimes will allow us to be tested, and allow bad things to happen even to good, faithful, church-going people. Indeed, even faithful people, those of us who walk by faith and not by sight, will face difficulties at certain points in life.

Earthquakes in Puerto Rico can't be fully explained in the context of our faithfulness. Hurricanes in New Orleans, Texas, Florida and Puerto Rico can't be fully explained in the context of our faithfulness. Wildfires in Australia, can't be fully explained. Tsunamis in South Asia can't be fully explained within the context of our faithfulness. Global pandemics of illness and suffering can't be fully explained. It can't be fully explained within the context of our faith in God why people get shot and killed on our city streets, why mass murders occur, and why other evil acts are inflicted on God's people.

Even faithful people sometimes find themselves going through challenging times. Even faithful people like you and me sometimes find ourselves between rocks and hard places, facing difficulties and distress, vicissitudes and valleys, trials and trouble, sorrow and suffering.

At points, all of us will be acquainted with the profoundly poetic words of the great bard Paul Laurence Dunbar –

A crust of bread and a corner to sleep in,

A minute to smile and an hour to weep in,
A pint of joy to a peck of trouble,
And never a laugh but the moans come double;
And that is life!

We'll all face challenges, we'll all be tested and tried, and our faith in God doesn't keep us from going through. Our faith doesn't make us immune to trials and tribulations, but what faith does for us is it gives us strength for the struggle, fortitude for the fight, and endurance amidst enmity and strife.

The Israelites did not lack faith, and God did not lack faithfulness toward them. But they found themselves going through.

So, what are lessons for us today in this psalm? What can we learn here for the living of the days that are ahead of us? What can our trials teach us?

- *First, we learn that we will all go through trials. That's the way of the world.*
- *Second, we learn that in the midst of trials, God will give us strength to endure.*
- *Third, we learn that as we walk by faith and not by sight, God will bring us out of every test and trial.*
- *Fourth, we learn that as we come out of a trial, as we come out of a test, we should come out thanking and praising God.*

Let's listen in on the psalmist and the people of God of his day as they praise God because *"God has preserved our lives and kept our feet from slipping"* (Psalm 66:9).

The good news is that God did not leave God's people alone in their trials. The psalmist ended with a shout of praise for what the Lord had done for them, how God had kept them, and brought them out. *"We went through the fire and water, but you (God) brought us to a place of abundance"* (Psalm 66:12). After all they went through, God brought them not to just any place, but God brought them and restored them to a place where there was plenty!

Good news for us is that, like the Israelites, we might go through proverbial fire and water, we might likewise go through seasons of trouble and difficulty, we might be tested and tried, but the Lord can and will bring us out! And when we come out, God can and will bring us to a place of abundance.

Ask the Savior to help you
Comfort, strengthen and keep you
He is able to aid you,
Jesus will carry you through.
(H. R. Palmer)

22 - WE CAN DEPEND ON GOD

In you, Lord, I have taken refuge; let me never be put to shame. In your righteousness, rescue me and deliver me; turn your ear to me and save me. Be my rock of refuge, to which I can always go; give the command to save me, for you are my rock and my fortress. Deliver me, my God, from the hand of the wicked, from the grasp of those who are evil and cruel. For you have been my hope, Sovereign Lord, my confidence since my youth. From birth I have relied on you; you brought me forth from my mother's womb. I will ever praise you." *(Psalm 71:1-6)*

All of us have been in places, spaces and situations in life where we have realized that we could not make it on our own. Some of us have been there lately.

Psalm 71 was written by somebody who had been acquainted with apparent helplessness and hopelessness. The psalmist had enough sense to acknowledge that, indeed, he had been at the place of needing help, and in the midst of it, he had cried out for help.

Here, we discover that it is one thing to have needed help, and it is yet another thing to have acknowledged that we were at the place of needing help. And it is one thing to cry out to the Lord when we're in trouble, but it is something else to look back when we're on the other side of trouble, and realize that the Lord, God almighty has brought us out and over the trouble we were in, and that we can depend on God.

Many people not only don't want to acknowledge that they've been in trouble and have needed help, but they also don't want to acknowledge that it was the Lord who brought them out of the trouble they were in.

The psalmist began this song by singing about a plethora of trouble spots, rough patches and problem places he'd endured in his life. In the first three verses, he sang about needing to be rescued, he talked about needing to be delivered, and he talked about needing to be saved. Furthermore, he talked about needing the Lord to be his rock of refuge (protection for him).

And the psalmist concluded his petitions and pleas for God's help in verse four when he prayed, *"Deliver me, my God, from the hand of the wicked, from the grasp of those who are evil and cruel"* (Psalm 71:4).

Certainly, many of us can sense the psalmist's pain. We can feel the deep disappointment, dire despair and dreadful desperation in his words. We can feel the realness and rawness of his plea for the Lord's rescue, relief and refuge. We can feel his cry for protection from his enemies, those wicked people and tough situations that had almost taken him out. We can feel the psalmist's fear and trepidation.

Indeed, many people today are at the place of crying out. We cry out amidst wars in too many parts of the world – Syria, Iraq, Afghanistan and Israel, among others. We cry out amidst the tragedy of COVID-19, which has affected and afflicted so many of our sisters and brothers in America and around the world. We cry out amidst lingering tragic diseases like Ebola, Malaria and HIV-AIDS, which have affected our sisters and brothers in Liberia, Sierra Leone, Nigeria, Ghana, and other parts of the world. We cry out amidst the violence that is wiping out too many of our young and destroying too many families and communities.

We cry out for those who are the victims of domestic violence and human trafficking. We cry out amidst abject poverty around the world. We cry out for our sisters and brothers who lack clean water, adequate food and safe shelter. We cry out for immigrant children at America's borders, and parents who have been separated from their children. We cry out to God for all among us who suffer.

We cry out to God for healing in our pain, provision in our need, peace in our turmoil, safety in our fears. We cry to the Lord.

Sometimes we hurt and we cry, and the world doesn't seem to know or hear that we're crying. The poetic words of Langston Hughes speak to our individual and communal cries –

Because my mouth
Is wide with laughter
And my throat
Is deep with song,
You do not think
I suffer
After I have held my pain
So long.

Because my mouth
Is wide with laughter
You do not hear
My inner cry?
Because my feet...
Are gay with dancing...

You do not know
I die?
(Minstrel Man)

And so, what assurance do we have amidst our bitter tears? We rest with the blessed assurance that as we cry to God, God indeed has listening ears that are inclined to hear us. In the psalmist's experience, we find the dynamics of our faith at work in three ways that can help us when we cry.

First, it is a natural and reasonable act of faith to cry to God when we are in trouble, hurting and afraid. Our tears are a sign that we know that there are some things in life that only God can and will handle, and bring us through. There are some problems that only God can solve, situations only God can fix.

There are some times when all we can do is, as the song-writer says – *"Have a little talk with Jesus and tell him all about our struggle..."*

Second, as the psalmist experienced, we can be assured that God hears our cries, whatever they are, and God will answer us. It's good to know that we worship and serve a prayer-answering God. It's good to know that our tears - however long they have fallen, however bitter they may be - are only temporary. God specializes in wiping away tears. God specializes in answering prayers, and coming to see about us. The psalmist's words ring true for us, *"Weeping may endure for a night, but joy comes in the morning"* (Psalm 30:5).

The song-writer wrote *".... He'll hear our faintest cry, and answer by and by..."*

Third, we can live with confidence in knowing that God who answers prayers will meet us at the points of our pain and

105

fears, and won't leave us there. God can and will strengthen our souls and give us the boldness to face and overcome our fears.

"... And just a little talk with Jesus, makes it right..."

Maybe the psalmist knew that he was praying this prayer not only for himself, and not only for people in his worship context over two millennia ago, but that there would be some people in 2020 who needed words of assurance and hope that we can likewise depend on God.

Maybe the psalmist knew that wickedness and oppression would exist in our world today, as it did then. Maybe he knew that hate would come against people today, as it did then. Maybe he knew that the evil and cruelty of his day would be similar to the evil and cruelty of today.

So, he declared to the Lord, *"From birth I have relied on you; you brought me forth from my mother's womb. I will ever praise you"* (Psalm 71:6). We are reminded of the same today.

It's good to know that we can depend on God. If we were to do inventory of our lives, think back on times and places when and where we've needed the Lord, and count our blessings for the times when the Lord showed up, we would conclude that at every juncture along the way, God has been there –

Through thick and thin – God's been there.
Come hell or high waters – God's been there.
Through ups and downs - the Lord has been there.

Through joy and pain - God's been there.
Through sunshine and rain - God's been there.

I love the Lord,
God heard my cry,
and pitied every groan...
As long as I live,
and trouble rise,
I'll hasten to God's throne.
(Richard Smallwood)

23 - THERE IS A BLESSING IN THIS

The Lord said to Moses, "Tell Aaron and his sons, 'This is how you are to bless the Israelites. Say to them: "The Lord bless you and keep you; the Lord make God's face shine on you and be gracious to you; the Lord turn God's face toward you and give you peace."' "So, they will put my name on the Israelites, and I will bless them." (Numbers 6:22-27)

I will bless the Lord at all times: God's praise shall continually be in my mouth. My soul shall make her boast in the Lord: the humble shall hear thereof, and be glad. O magnify the Lord with me, and let us exalt God's name together. I sought the Lord, and God heard me, and delivered me from all my fears. (Psalm 34:1-4)

As we look back over the past year (2020), and reflect on everything that has occurred, and frankly, all that has *gone wrong* for many of us, individually and communally, we have to ask ourselves, "Where is the good in any of it? Where is the blessing in any of it? What good has come out of the last year that can help us lean and live more hopefully into 2021?"

I realize that we believe by faith that God is a God of blessing, that God is a God who wills and desires good and well-being for our lives, but how does this square with the existential pain and suffering, and nihilistic loss that so many of God's people, even many of us who walk by faith and not by sight, have experienced?

The truth of the matter is that it is difficult to see blessing in the midst of burden. And the bigger the burden, the more difficult it is often to see, experience and talk about blessing. And yet, there is indeed a blessing imbedded in any and everything we must go through and endure in this life.

That is the point of Lord's instructions to Moses in Numbers 6: *The Lord said to Moses, "Tell Aaron and his sons, 'This is how you are to bless the Israelites. Say to them: "The Lord bless you and keep you; the Lord make God's face shine on you and be gracious to you; the Lord turn God's face toward you and give you peace."' "So, they will put my name on the Israelites, and I will bless them"* (v. 22-27).

The Israelites had gone through some difficulties and distress. They had faced the devastating despair of 430 years of slavery at the hands of Egypt. They had just come out of 10 plagues, and years of destruction had ripped at their lives, as it did Pharaoh and the Egyptians. Israel, God's people, had wandered in the wilderness for 40 years, often wondering what they would eat and drink, and where they would lay their heads.

And, in the midst of it, all God wanted Moses to tell Aaron and his sons to tell Israel is that *the Lord would bless them and keep them.* The people of God needed to be reminded that in and through everything they had experienced, God had somehow, someway made a way for them to get through, and that God would do the same in the days ahead.

They needed a reminder that the same God who had blessed them to survive slavery, the same God who had blessed them with deliverance at the Red Sea, the same God who had rained down food and water in the wilderness - is the same God who would bless and keep them in generations to come.

In other words, Israel needed a reminder that there were blessings imbedded in everything they had gone through.

Likewise, as difficult as days have been for us, as dire as times have gotten for many of us, the Lord's instructions to

Moses for Aaron and his sons, and the same prayer of blessing for Israel, has our name on it today - *"The Lord bless you and keep you, the Lord make God's face shine on you and be gracious to you."*

There is a blessing in this. *"The Lord bless you and keep you."* Some of us can testify that the Lord has been a keeper and comforter through everything we've gone through lately. Some of us have a testimony that God has been our help and hope in the midst of it all. Some of us can attest to the fact that God has been our peace in every one of life's storms. Some of us can testify that God has brought us over every mountain we've had to climb, and seen us through every valley we've found ourselves in.

There's blessing in this. Now, we can look back over 2020, and think about where we've been, and all that we've gone through. We don't know how we made it, there may have been points when many of us did not think that we would make it, but we've made it. There may have been days when we wanted to give up, quit, throw in the towel and tap out on life, but God has kept us.

There's a blessing in this. And if God blessed us through what we've gone through, God will bless us in whatever it is that will come our way today and tomorrow.

And we are reminded that the blessing in this doesn't stop with God blessing us. In Psalm 34, the psalmist declared, *"I will bless the Lord at all times, God's praises shall continually be in my mouth"* (v.1).

The psalmist said, *"I will bless the Lord at all times."* "With whatever my circumstances, I will bless the Lord. In tough and terrible times, I will bless the Lord. In trouble and tumult, I will bless the Lord. In trials and tribulations, I will bless the Lord. In pandemic and pandemonium, I will bless God. In valleys and vicissitudes, I will bless God."

There's a blessing in this. "In joy and pain, sunshine and rain, good and bad, in up and down, I will bless God."

How could the psalmist share such a testimony, and how might we? Because when we look back over all that's happened, we realize that if it had not been for the Lord who was on our side, we don't know where we would be.

How? Because, when we look back over our lives, and think things over, we can truly say that in and through it all, we've been blessed. We've got a testimony.

There is a blessing even in this. When I think of the goodness of Jesus, and all that the Lord has done for me (us), my soul shouts hallelujah, I thank God for blessing me (us)!

Blessed assurance, Jesus is mine,
O what a foretaste of glory divine.
Heir of salvation, purchased of God.
Born of his spirit, washed in his blood.
This is my story. This is my song.
Praising my Savior, all the days long.
This is my story. This is my song.
Praising my Savior, all the day long.
(Fannie Crosby)

SECTION III
SONGS OF HOPE
(HOPE SINGS!)

24 - THIS IS A NEW DAY!

This is the day that the Lord has made; let us rejoice and be glad in it. (Psalm 118:24)

In every generation, it is the task of the church to reflect upon what it has been, what it is, and what it is that God calls it to become.

For persons of faith in ancient times, remembrance was often an opportunity for recollecting on the past – a time of reminiscence about what God had done in their lives. But remembrance was also a time of looking to the future in light of what God had done - with expectancy as to what God was about to do in and for the people. The Greek notion of *anamnesis* is most evident in this kind of remembrance – where we are simultaneously looking back at the past and looking forward to the future.

Some theologians have suggested that the church is a people of both the "right now" and the "not yet" – or the yet to be. This is the eschatological hope that we share in Christ, who is the *resurrection and the life.* Ours is a faith that is yet being fulfilled in this life. We are a pilgrim people, on a journey of faith and discipleship to those places and spaces where God is yet leading us.

We come together to reflect upon the past – what God has done in, through and for us – and to look to the future to see what God is about to do in our lives.

As those of ancient times would gather to remember, each of us today has a story to tell of how God has met us. And so it is that we gather today with memories of the past, and hopes for the future.

Endings and beginnings are seldom easy – for they insinuate change. Amidst the inevitability and reality of change, we often find ourselves pondering the question," Is the cup of life half empty, or is it half full?"

I want to suggest that for people of faith, the cup of life is always both half empty and half full. With change – with new beginnings – with new days - comes new opportunities and challenges, new possibilities and promise, new and exciting ways for us to experience God in our future. We are a people of hope – and indeed this is a new day.

This is the encouragement that we find in the words of the psalmist, who said,
> *"This is the day that the Lord has made, let us rejoice and be glad in it"* (Psalm 118:4).

Eugene Peterson in *The Message* reframed (remixed) this passage this way:
> *"This is the very day GOD acted. Let's celebrate and be festive."*

Indeed, we can rejoice, celebrate and be glad today knowing that God has created a brand new day for us, with brand new possibilities. We can rejoice, celebrate and be glad because we are confident that God offers us new opportunities – new and exciting ways of being. Indeed, as the prophet Jeremiah declared, ours is *a future filled with hope* (Jeremiah 29:11).

And so, the words of song-writer Brian Wren are appropriate for us:
> *This is a day of new beginnings*
> *Time to remember and move on*

Time to believe what love is bringing
Laying to rest the pain that's gone.

Then let us with the Spirit's daring
Step from the past and leave behind
This is a day of new beginnings
Our God is making all things new.

In faith we'll gather round the table
To taste and share what love can do
This is a day of new beginnings
Our God is making all things new.

It remains our awesome task as the church to live faithfully and hopefully into the new day that God has given us. And it will be our faith and hope in God that will sustain us, strengthen us, encourage us, and lead us into the future with hope.

Indeed, it has been our faith that has sustained us, and this same faith will be with us.

God (has been) our help in ages past,
(and God is) our hope for years to come.
(God has been) our shelter from the stormy blast,
(God is) our eternal home.
(Isaac Watts)

O that God would continue to lead us and guide us in this new day. And O that we would look to the days ahead with trust and faith in God who has created us.

I do not know how long 'twill be

115

Or what the future holds for (you and) me
But this I know,
If Jesus leads (us)
We'll get home someday.
(Charles Albert Tindley)

25 - A RIGHT-POSITIONED HOPE

I said, "I will watch my ways and keep my tongue from sin; I will put a muzzle on my mouth while in the presence of the wicked." So, I remained utterly silent, not even saying anything good. But my anguish increased; my heart grew hot within me. While I meditated, the fire burned; then I spoke with my tongue: "Show me, Lord, my life's end and the number of my days; let me know how fleeting my life is." You have made my days a mere handbreadth; the span of my years is as nothing before you. Everyone is but a breath, even those who seem secure. Surely everyone goes around like a mere phantom; in vain they rush about, heaping up wealth without knowing whose it will finally be. But now, Lord, what do I look for? My hope is in you. (Psalm 39:1-7)

Sickness and sorrow, sadness and suffering - these are things that can burden us to the point of *unbelieving thoughts*, and even near *faithlessness and near hopelessness.* If we are truthful, these things may lead us to the inability to pray, and lead us out of proximity with God.

It really doesn't matter who we are, from where we've come, where we've gone to school, where we live, how much money we may or may not have in the bank - storms of life can and will come into our lives, and disturb us, mess us up, and turn life topsy-turvy.

Soul singer, Marvin Gaye, placed the existential realities of the challenges that we face into context in his 1971 song, "What's Going On":

Mother, mother
There's too many of you crying
Brother, brother, brother
There's far too many of you dying
You know we've got to find a way
To bring some lovin' here today - Ya

Father, father
We don't need to escalate
You see, war is not the answer
For only love can conquer hate
You know we've got to find a way
To bring some lovin' here today

Picket lines and picket signs
Don't punish me with brutality
Talk to me, so you can see
Oh, what's going on
What's going on
Yeah, what's going on
Ah, what's going on.

What's going on? Perennial questions in times like these are, "Where is God in the midst of our going through? What is the efficacy and effectuality of our faith? Where might we find hope?"

This was the place and predicament of the psalmist in Psalm 39. This is a song of David who was nearing the end of his life, and reflecting on the meaning of all that he had gone through. It is, in many ways, a blues song, a sorrow song like our ancestors would sing in centuries past, a song like, *"Nobody knows the trouble I've seen... Nobody knows my sorrow..."*

In Psalm 38, the psalmist, David, looked back over his life and wrote about being sick, *"Because of your wrath there is no health in my body; there is no soundness in my bones because of my sin"* (Psalm 38:3).

And here in Psalm 39, in part-two of this song, David was looking at the prospect of his final days. *"Show me, Lord, my life's end and the number of my days; let me know how fleeting my life is"* (v. 4).

David's reckoning with his human frailty and finitude can help those of us who are going through any form of difficulty today, and help us with what we might go through tomorrow. He was like you, me, and everybody else who is trying to walk by faith and not by sight. David was like everybody else who is trying to maintain faith and find hope in the midst of existential darkness, despair and distress.

David had been faithful, he had been prayerful, he had been full of worship and praise, and he loved God with his whole heart. But David now found himself facing the realities of life and death, of going through. And not just going through, but he was going through to the point of wanting to give up on God, and on life.

If we pay close attention, we can sense David's despair. We can empathize with him. What's the use of faith for immigrant mothers and fathers separated from their children at America's borders? What good is faith for the 348 families whose loved ones were murdered in Baltimore city in 2019, or for the 50 families who lost loved ones to murder in Baltimore County in 2019? What good is faith for persons who slept on grates last night, and those who will have nothing to eat today?

What good is faith for those who are sick, and have no healthcare?

Our ancestors could relate to such challenges, and James Weldon Johnson poetically captured them in the second verse of his great song, "Life Every Voice and Sing" –

> *Stony the road we trod,*
> *bitter the chast'ning rod,*
> *felt in the day that hope*
> *unborn had died;*
> *yet with a steady beat,*
> *have not our weary feet,*
> *come to the place*
> *on which our fathers sighed?*

David's predicament is a reminder for us that we might get to the place in life where we, likewise, wonder "what's the use?" Life deals us blow after blow, difficulty after difficulty, trial after trial, and we might be led to ask, "What's the use?" Troubles and tribulations come, valleys and vicissitudes meet us, despair and disappointments greet us, and we wonder, "Why?" Where is God in the midst of it all?" "What's the use?"

Indeed, David's song reminds us that there can be junctures in life where we realize that our faith does not make us immune to suffering. There might be points at which the songs that have encouraged us before won't suffice, the sermons that we've heard won't get us through, and even our prayers seem to be inadequate.

So, what then will help us? What do we, as people of faith, have at our disposal?

What we have at our disposal is hope. David concluded this section of Psalm 39 by helping us to see that at the end of it all, with everything we've gone through and may go through, we have a right-positioned hope. At the conclusion of his reckoning with God in Psalm 39, David shared an affirmation of his faith in the living God. *"But now, Lord, what do I look for? My hope is in you"* (v. 7). He had a right-positioned hope.

Dr. Martin Luther King, Jr. said in a 1967 sermon, "The Meaning of Hope", that *"Hope is the refusal to give up despite insurmountable odds."* In his book *A Gospel of Hope,* Dr. Walter Brueggemann writes that *"Hope is the deep religious conviction that God has not quit."*

Concerning hope, St. Augustine, the fourth century Bishop of Hippo, said that *"Hope has two beautiful daughters; their names are Anger and Courage. Anger at the way things are, and Courage to see that they do not remain as they are."* Hope does not settle for the status quo. Hope says that where there is suffering and difficulty, it does not suffice for people of faith to go along just to get along.

King further intimated that hope is always animated by our faith and love, and that if we have hope, we have faith in something.

At the end of it all, David said, *"But now, Lord, what do I look for? My hope is in you."* We learn from David that when it's all said and done, we, as people of faith, can be confident that our hope, likewise, is in the Lord. Indeed, what we as people of faith have in our spiritual arsenal is hope (if we don't have anything else).

Why? Because, regardless of how bad things are or how difficult days may become, Brueggemann was right - God has not quit. Hope says that God is not dead and God is not done!

Ours is a right-positioned hope. Such hope assures us that *"weeping may endure for a night, but joy comes in the morning" (Psalm 30:5).* Such hope assures us that *"the suffering of this present day is not worthy to be compared to the glory that will be revealed in us"* (Romans 8:18). Such hope helps walk in the assurance that *"all thigs work together for the good of those who love God and are called according to God's purpose"* (Romans 8:28).

What does a right-positioned hope look like?

> *Hope reminds us that God is not finished with any of us yet.*
>
> *Hope insists that "greater is God who is in us, than he who is in the world"* (1 John 4:4).
>
> *Hope says that "we can do all things through Christ who strengthens us"* (Philippians 4:13).
>
> *Hope helps us to know that we may not know what tomorrow holds, but we know who holds tomorrow.*
>
> *Hope woke us up this morning, and hope started us on our way.*
>
> *Hope put food on the table, and clothes on our backs.*
>
> *Hope clothed us in our right minds.*
>
> *Hope healed the sick, and hope raised the dead.*
>
> *Hope took two fish and five loaves of bread, and fed more than five thousand hungry people.*
>
> *Hope deliverers, redeems, satisfies, saves and sanctifies us.*

Our hope is in the Lord! A right-positioned hope is a hope that's alive. It's a hope that's not dead, dormant, drab, dreary or dull. It is not stagnant, stale, latent or vapid. A right-positioned hope beckons us to keep dreaming with an animated faith and tenacious love. Ours is a right-positioned hope, and might we hold to the lyrics of the great hymn –

My hope is built on nothing less
Than Jesus' blood and righteousness.
I dare not trust the sweetest frame
But wholly lean in Jesus's name.
On Christ the solid Rock I stand
All other ground is sinking sand.

When he shall come with trumpet sound
O may I then in him be found.
Dressed in his righteousness alone
Faultless to stand before the throne.
On Christ the solid rock I stand,
All other ground is sinking sand.
(Edward Mote)

26 - KEEP HOPING

In you, Lord my God, I put my trust. I trust in you; do not let me be put to shame, nor let my enemies triumph over me. No one who hopes in you will ever be put to shame, but shame will come on those who are treacherous without cause. Show me your ways, Lord, teach me your paths. Guide me in your truth and teach me, for you are God my Savior, and my hope is in you all day long. (Psalm 25:1-5)

Near the end of his life, Rev. Dr. Martin Luther King, Jr. published his final book entitled, *Where Do We Go from Here: Chaos or Community?* In it, he reiterated a point he had made on several other occasions. He pointed out that we are faced with a choice in our life together, and that we will either learn to live together as brothers and sisters, or we will die together as fools.

A part of the obligation of churches, civil and human rights organizations and all other institutions and persons concerned about the well-being of our world today remains that of speaking to the critical moral and social issues of the contemporary age. It is our task to help articulate a framework for engaging in critical and constructive advocacy for the disinherited among us – the poor, the violated, the marginalized, and the oppressed.

In light of this, where might hope reside among us as we look to the future? King framed his vision of hope within the context of his notion of the *Beloved Community*. In one of his later sermons, "The Meaning of Hope," he defined hope as that quality which is *"necessary for life."*

King asserted that hope was to be viewed as *"animated and undergirded by faith and love."* In his mind, if you had hope, you had faith in something. For King, hope was *"the refusal to give up despite overwhelming odds."* In his famous "I Have a Dream" speech delivered on the steps of the Lincoln Memorial in Washington, DC on August 28, 1963, King shared that a part of his dream was that we would be able *"to hew out of the mountain of despair, a stone of hope."*

With all that is going on in our world today, some would assert that it is difficult to locate God, and recognize what God is doing, what God is up to in our lives, and in the world. With all the noise and confusion in the atmosphere, it's often difficult to hear from the Lord, and see hope.

Some would argue that we are living in times when, in no small way, there's a paucity of hope - where a certain nihilism - a certain emptiness, lovelessness, lifelessness, nothingness, meaninglessness - and indeed an apparent hopelessness pervades and permeates the church and the world.

The neo-soul singer India Arie alluded to this in her song – *"There's Hope"*:
Gas prices - they just keep on rising (There's hope)
The government - they keep on lying
But we gotta keep on surviving...
Keep living our truth and do the best we can do.

I know some of us could say, "I hear you, India Arie. I know what you're talking about when you say, despite all that's going on, "we gotta keep on surviving."" "I hear you India, but if you know like I know sometimes hope seems like it's on a tight rope." Hope sometimes seems hard to see, hard to hold onto, and it's difficult to hang in, and keep on surviving.

In the midst of it all, what we, as people of faith need to remember is that we're not the first people who find ourselves living and surviving amidst a paucity of hope. The people in the world just prior to Jesus's birth were living in a similar state.

From Malachi to Matthew, the Bible shows us that hope had been silent for over 400 years. The people of the Lord's day had waited, and waited on God, to no apparent avail. They had waited on the Lord, and *all they could do was to keep on surviving. All they could do was keep hoping.*

What is it that can help us to keep hoping in times like these? In whom can we hope?

Let's listen in on the psalmist in Psalm 25. Here, David was singing the song of a people whose hope was on a tightrope. He was singing the song of a people who had gone through attacks by their enemies.

Let's consider the psalmist's lyrics – *"In you, Lord my God, I put my trust. I trust in you; do not let me be put to shame, nor let my enemies triumph over me. No one who hopes in you will ever be put to shame, but shame will come on those who are treacherous without cause."*

David ended this song by declaring that *"my hope is in you, God, all day long."* We are likewise beckoned to place our hope, and our future, in God's hands.

In Jeremiah 29:11, the prophet offered a hopeful vision for a people experiencing exile in a strange land. Here, the Israelites were in Babylon – alienated from their land, alienated from God, and alienated – many of them - from their loved

126

ones. It is against this backdrop of near hopelessness that Jeremiah shared these words of hope:

> *"For surely, I know the plans I have for you, says the Lord, plans for your welfare (shalom, wholeness, well-being), and not for your harm, plans to give you a future with hope."*

Those were the same times that would lead Jeremiah earlier to offer provocative questions with the same people –

"Is there no balm in Gilead? Is there no healing there? Why then has the health of my people not been restored?" (Jer. 8:22)

In reflecting on this text from Jeremiah, Dr. Martin Luther King, Jr. pointed out that evidence of faith and hope is found in the fact that Blacks who were enslaved and oppressed in America in centuries past were able to convert the *question mark* of the prophet Jeremiah's lament, to an *exclamation point* as they affirmed their faith and hope in the living and life-giving God in a song:

There is a balm in Gilead,
To make the wounded whole
There is a balm in Gilead,
To heal the sin-sick soul.
Sometimes I feel discouraged
And think my work's in vain.
And then the Holy Spirit
Revives my soul again!

The encouragement for us is to keep hoping. Hope beckons us to love everybody – both our allies and enemies. Hope helps us to see that we can resist giving up on one another because our lives together are animated by the belief that God is present in each and every one of us. Hope helps us to believe that God is the orchestrator of grace, mercy and justice for all people.

Hope can be found in the possibilities that we will continue to discover ways to capitalize on those experiences and encounters that will lead to us being intentional and inclusive community. This is the hope that must be realized if we are to be the *Beloved Community* that Martin Luther King, Jr. imagined, and that God wills.

In the days ahead, may we continue to muster the audacity to see visions and dream dreams, and may we have the temerity to hope against all that seems to rise and push against hope. May we have the courage to hold onto hope.

And even when our hopes and dreams seem to be nearly dashed, destroyed and nullified, may we muster the courage to heed the sentiments of the great bard Langston Hughes –

Hold fast to dreams
For if dreams die
Life is a broken-winged bird
That cannot fly.

Hold fast to dreams
For when dreams go
Life is a barren field
Frozen with snow.

27 - OUR DROUGHT WILL END

When you, God, went out before your people, when you marched through the wilderness, the earth shook, the heavens poured down rain, before God, the One of Sinai, before God, the God of Israel. You gave abundant showers, O God; you refreshed your weary inheritance. Your people settled in it, and from your bounty, God, you provided for the poor. (Psalm 68:7-10)

Every person goes through times of existential drought, or dry seasons in life. These are the times when we don't see the changes we hoped for, the times when things might not seem to be going our way, the times when God might seem far off.

We've got big dreams, we're standing on God's promises, we're keeping the faith, but things stay the same. Life is stagnant, staid and stale. It's a dry and barren season in our lives. We're in an existential drought.

We may even be blessed in one area of life, but find ourselves in a drought in another area. In these circumstances, it is easy to think, "This is the way it's always going to be. I'll always have this struggle. Things are so dry for me, and I've experienced this drought for so long, that it feels like things will never get better."

But what God wants us to know is that whatever our drought is, and however long it has lasted, it is about to come to an end. The promise that we stand on today is that the God we serve specializes in drought remediation, and God is waiting to step into our situation - whatever and wherever it is – however complex and convoluted our situation may be. God can and God will turn things around.

How do we know? This is the affirmation that the palmist David made in his song in Psalm 69. With all that David had gone through, with all that he was going through – and with all that the people of Israel had experienced in their faith journey, David needed to remind them and to remind himself about the God that they served, who God is, and what God does.

And so, in his time of need and despair, David prayed to God, and affirmed that *"You gave abundant showers, O God."* Whatever the need had been, David could affirm that God, who knows all and is our all-in-all, had sent exactly what he and the people needed, exactly when they needed it. Amidst their drought, God sent abundant showers, plentiful rain.

And whatever the drought has been for us, we can likewise testify today that God has stepped in and sent abundant showers, plentiful rain our way. Sickness in our bodies – God has stepped in. Death on our doorsteps – God has stepped in. Relationship problems – God has stepped in. Money problems - God has stepped in. Oppression, depression or whatever else it has been for us - God has stepped in.

When we've needed it, God has sent abundant showers, and if God did it before, God can and will do it again. And so, we can be assured, and declare with confidence that whatever our drought may be – it will end. In any area of dryness, despair, brokenness, loneliness, and in every empty place - if we keep the faith, God is going to rain down favor, grace, mercy, healing, forgiveness, restoration, reconciliation, redemption, deliverance, blessing, provision and hope on our lives.

As the psalmist could attest, this season is one where the people of God – you and me – will see abundant showers, plentiful rain (if we keep the faith)!

Indeed, every drought is only temporary. Dry seasons don't last forever. The song-writer was right, "Trouble don't last always." Struggle and lack are not our destiny. They are temporary. Our drought – whatever it is, and however long it lasts – will end.

It's good to know that abundant showers – plentiful rain - is headed our way!

So, let's be encouraged to declare by faith, "God, thank you that our drought is about to end, and that we will see abundant showers of your goodness and joy in our lives!" Jesus said, *"I've come that you may have life, and have it more abundantly"* (John 10:10).

Let's thank God for reigning in our lives, and raining down strength to stand strong as God's plan unfolds for our lives in Jesus' name.

Let's thank God for refreshing, renewing and regenerating rain on every dry place in our lives. Let's thank God for raining down provision, blessing, hope, wisdom, joy, peace and unconditional love.

Let's thank God for the promise that our drought will end!

There shall be showers of blessing:
 This is the promise of love;
There shall be seasons refreshing,
 Sent from the Savior above.

 Showers of blessing,
  Showers of blessing we need;
 Mercy-drops round us are falling,
  But for the showers we plead.

C. Anthony Hunt

("There Shall be Showers of Blessing", D. W. Whittle)

28 - LET GO, LET GOD

As for me, I call to God, and the Lord saves me. Evening, morning and noon I cry out in distress, and God hears my voice. God rescues me unharmed from the battle waged against me, even though many oppose me. God, who is enthroned from of old, who does not change— God will hear them and humble them, because they have no fear of God. My companion attacks his friends; he violates his covenant. His talk is smooth as butter, yet war is in his heart; his words are more soothing than oil, yet they are drawn swords. Cast your cares on the Lord and God will sustain you; God will never let the righteous be shaken. (Psalm 55:16-22)

A common human proclivity and propensity amidst human distress is to worry. In despair, it is a reasonable human response for us to hold on to uncertainty, and in the midst of apparent hopelessness, to wonder and worry about the future.

As this is so in the midst of the pandemic times in which we now find ourselves, it was also the case in days almost three millennia ago when the psalmist was writing this song. As we listen in on the psalmist, David, we hear that he was singing a song in the midst of a blues season he was in, or a blues season out of which he had just come.

How do we know? We know because David starts this song by talking about crying out to God in distress. We know that reasonable people don't go around singing about crying out to God in distress unless we've actually been at a point of needing to cry out to God. This is to say that we cry, shed bitter tears, for reasons. We cry because we have reasons to do so.

Many of us can relate to David's song about crying out in distress. We know what it's like to have to cry out. We know well what uncertainty, fear and doubt feels like. We know about crying out amidst seemingly unending racism and sexism, marginalization and oppression.

We know what worry about our health, worry about our loved ones, worry about our finances, worry about our children and grandchildren, and worry about what tomorrow will be like for us feels like.

We can relate to David's bitter tears, and his crying out to the Lord - as he said – that he cried out *evening, morning and noon* (that's a lot of crying out). We can relate to feeling, at times, like the world is against us.

We can relate to times, when we have felt like we've needed God to come and rescue us. We can relate in some ways to wondering what will be the way out of the mess that we're in. We can relate to wondering, in the midst of things falling apart around us, if, when and how God will put our lives back together.

We can relate to crying out. And we might wonder what remedy God has for us in the midst of distress, worry and wonder.

David gave us an answer in Psalm 55:22 - *"cast your cares on the Lord, and God will sustain you."*

In other words, after all that he and the people had gone through, after all of the distress and despair that had been theirs, after all the rain and pain that had come into their lives, David's wise advice to them was to *cast their cares on the Lord.*

In other words, there come times in the lives of people who walk by faith and not by sight that we need to know that *it's alright to let go, and let God.*

How in the world could David tell the people to *cast their cares on the Lord?* How could he encourage them to *let go, and let God?* David could encourage them because of what he knew the Lord had done for him. He could encourage the people to *let go, and let God* because God had heard David's cries, and pitied his every groan.

David could encourage them to *let go, and let God* because God had made ways out of no way in his life and the people's lives before. God had shown up over and over again, and God had rescued them, provided for them and sustained them.

David could encourage them to *let go, and let God* because he knew that *if it had not been for the Lord who was on their side, he didn't know where they would be* (Psalm 124:1). He could encourage them to *let go, and let God* because, as he declared in another psalm, *"I've been young, and I've been old, but I've never seen the righteous forsaken, or God's seed begging for bread"* (Psalm 37:25).

And what God did for David, God will do the same for us. If God has done it before, God will do it again.

Indeed, when we know what God has done for us before, we can rest assured in our faith that the same God who did it then, will do it again. David's encouragement, and the same encouragement of Peter some 2000 years ago is ours today, we can *"cast all our cares on (Christ), for he cares for us"* (1 Peter 5:7).

David's plea is a word for you and me, with whatever we are going through today. Let's be encouraged to *cast our cares on the Lord, because God cares for us.* God will sustain us. Whatever our cares may be, let's be encouraged to *let go, and let God.*

Be not dismayed, whatever betide

135

C. Anthony Hunt

God will take care of you
Beneath God's wings of love abide
God will take care of you.

God will take care of you
Through everyday o'er all the way
God will care for you
God will take care of you.
(Civilla Durfee Martin)

29 - KEEP YOURS EYES ON THE PRIZE

I lift up my eyes to the mountains— where does my help come from? My help comes from the LORD, the Maker of heaven and earth. (Psalm 121:1-2)

One thing we have learned amidst the multiple pandemics that we have journeyed through lately is that it can be difficult to discern and to determine where to place our focus in times of distress.

Indeed, it can be difficult to focus when pandemics and pandemonium are our lot. There are so many "trees" of concern that it is often difficult to see the "forest". Whatever our vision is – it can be blurred in the midst of it all.

Indeed, we are dealing with multiple pandemics right now – in the church and in the world. We are dealing with the pandemic of COVID-19 (and health crises), the pandemic of racism, xenophobia and white supremacy, and the pandemic of economic despair for millions of Americans and millions more people around the world.

We are dealing with the pandemic of racialized police brutality and violence that is disproportionately directed at Black and Brown persons. We are dealing with the pandemic of political and partisan discord that – in no small ways – has threatened to paralyze American democracy.

We are dealing with a pandemic of untruth and incivility – where lies and deceit have – in no small ways - been normalized, and where loving and respecting our neighbors (and our enemies) is too often lacking among us. Indeed, pandemics of any type and in any season can cause us to lose focus.

We can sense that the psalmist in Psalm 121 was speaking of similar experiences. We find here a Song of Ascent, where the Israelites were looking up to God, and headed to their place of worship. The psalmist offered words of personal testimony, and began by declaring, *"I lift up my eyes to the mountains."* He had set his eyes above himself and his situation; he was looking beyond himself and his circumstances, outside his own experience. In another translation it says, *"I set my eyes to the hills."*

When have there been times in our lives when we have been like the psalmist, and needed to look up to God – look beyond ourselves to get what we need, and to get to where we want to go? There are times in each of our lives when we will meet with situations and circumstances that we can't handle on our own. There are some problems that we can't fix, mountains that we can't climb on our own, and valleys that we can't come out of by ourselves. It's good to know that we who walk by faith and not by sight can look beyond ourselves for help when we need it.

Then the psalmist proceeded to ask a question that he then proceeded to answer – *"From where does my help come? My help comes from the Lord, the Maker of heaven and earth."* As people of God, people of faith, we likewise rest with the certainty that our help is in the Lord. We live with the assurance that when we look up, God is going to show up. That is why the psalmist could reiterate in another Song of Ascent, *"Our help is in the name of the Lord, the Maker of heaven and earth"* (Psalm 124:8).

We are encouraged to keep our eyes on the prize. We know that the greater the challenge, the more focused we need to be on God. We are encouraged to keep looking up to God, from where our help comes. For, we know that the greater the trial, the greater is our need to focus on God who made heaven and earth.

The 20th century soul prophets, Earth, Wind and Fire, encourage us with their song, "Keep Your Head to the Sky":

Master told me one day
I'd find peace in every way
But in search for the clue
Wrong things I was bound to do
Keep my head to the sky
For the clouds to tell me why
As I grew, and with strength
Master kept me as I repent
And he said!

Keep your head to the sky
Keep your head to the sky.

The late hip hop artist Tupac Shakur offered similar words of encouragement – *"Keep your head up... things are going to get easier."*

And so, what might such vision entail? Such vision entails three components - *hindsight, insight, and foresight.*

Our hindsight helps us to look back and see what's happened in our past. Hindsight helps us to consider how God has brought us through dangers, toils and snares before. In our

139

hindsight, we might sing as the psalmist sang in another place, *"If it had not been for the Lord who was on our side, where would we be?"* (Psalm 124:1) Hindsight might lead us to sing with a testimony of praise, *"When I look back over my life and think things over, I can truly say that I've been blessed. I've got a testimony."*

Hindsight helps us recognize that God has been our help in ages past, and will be our hope for days to come. Indeed, if God brought the Israelites through, and brought our parents through, won't God do the same and bring us through?

Our insight helps us to see where we are right now. Insight helps us to recognize how, when and where God is at work in our lives. It helps us to realize that God is a very present help in all of our times of trouble. With insight we can see what God is doing right now in our lives, and realize that God is an on-time, all the time, every time, everywhere God.

Our hindsight and insight – what God has done and what God is doing – gives vision, hope, anticipation and expectation of what God will do in our lives, and gives impetus to our foresight. *Foresight helps us anticipate how God will make ways in our future.* It helps us see that God intends to heal us, provide for us, redeem us and save us. It helps us to know, as Jeremiah knew, that God indeed has a plan for each and every one of us, and that God's divine intent is not that we would be harmed, but that we would be well, and that God will give us *a future with hope* (Jeremiah 29:11).

Let's be encouraged to keep our eyes on the prize. Let's keep looking up to the hills where we will find our help. Let's pray like everything depends on God, and let's work like everything depends on us. Let's keep looking up, believing beyond belief that the God of all grace and glory is going to show up.   God's faithfulness toward us is indeed great... *strength for today, and bright hope for tomorrow.*

30 - MIND YOUR MANNERS

Praise the Lord! O give thanks to the Lord, for God is good, for God's steadfast love endures forever. Who can utter the mighty doings of the Lord, or declare all God's praise? (Psalm 106:1-2)

In everything give thanks, for this is the will of God concerning you. (1 Thess. 5:18)

In the beginning verse of Psalm 106, the psalmist encouraged those who would hear with these words, *"O give thanks to the Lord, for God is good; God's steadfast love endures forever.*

This was a word of reminder to the faithful of that day. In order that their faith might be well-founded and properly grounded, in order that their hope and perspective might be sustained, the psalmist offered the people of God a lesson in thanksgiving. In order to improve their aptitude for praise and enhance their attitude of gratitude, the psalmist offered words of instruction as to the conditions in which the believers of his day were to render their appreciation, and say *"thank you"* to the Lord.

These ancient words of reminder are as important for us today as they were for the people of God almost three millennia ago. It has been suggested that there is an infectious disease that continues to permeate our land. It is the disease of ingratitude. We live in an age where many people have forgotten how to say *"thank you."* Ingratitude has subsumed us.

There is a certain irony that can be found here, in that we are in many ways more blessed than we have ever been in the history of civilization. We are blessed with technological advances and material things that our parents and grandparents could have only dreamt about.

Many of us are blessed to have finer homes, larger cars and more expensive clothing than we ever thought we should or could possess. Many of us are blessed to be more educated and to have better jobs than we ever thought possible. We're blessed.

But still, many people today are infected with the disease of ingratitude. For some reason many people are ungrateful, and seem not to know how to say *"thank you."*

I remember growing up, and being taught as one of the first lessons of life how to say *"please"* when I wanted something, and *"thank you"* when I got it. It was engrained into us as young people that if we wanted somebody to do something for us, we'd first need to say *"please."* And once somebody was kind enough to do something for us, however small or large it was, the appropriate response was to say *"thank you."*

In other words, it was engrained in us to *mind our manners*, and to demonstrate an attitude of gratitude.

The psalmist said, *"O give thanks to the Lord, for God is good; God's steadfast love endures forever."*

In similar words of encouragement, the apostle Paul wrote to the church at Thessalonica and said, *"In everything give thanks, for this is the will of God concerning you"* (1 Thessalonians 5:18).

What Paul was saying to the congregation in Thessalonica is that the zenith of Christian conduct is to be able to say *"thank you"* in all circumstances. *"In everything give thanks"*, Paul said.

Here, in I Thessalonians we find that Paul was en-route to Rome with a layover in Corinth when he wrote his first letter to the young church at Thessalonica. Paul was aware that the church there would have its ups and downs, its risings and fallings. Above all else, it is apparent that the people in the midst of whatever they were going through had forgotten how to say *"thank you"* to the Lord.

And so, Paul encouraged them by telling them that they were to give thanks in all things. Herein lays the real challenge of faith and life. If we are to follow Paul's instruction, we will develop the capacity to give thanks for the good and the bad situations of life. We will be able to give thanks in ups as well as in downs, in joy and pain, in sunshine and rain, in life and in death, in success and sorrows, in triumph and in trials, in valleys and vicissitudes. Paul says, *"In all things give thanks."*

We are encouraged to *mind our manners* before God, and give God thanks and praise in all situations, for all that the Lord has done, and is doing for us.

Bishop Yvette Flunder and Bishop Walter Hawkins encourage us with their song, *"Thank You, Lord"*:

Tragedies are common place
All kinds of diseases, people are slipping away

Economies down, people can't get enough pay
As for me all I can say is
Thank you Lord
for all you've done for me.

The psalmist declared, *"Give thanks to the Lord, for the Lord is good; for God's steadfast love endures forever."*

Mind your manners.

Why? Because it's good to acknowledge that the Lord is good in all things and in all ways.

- From the rising of the sun, to the going down of the same, *God is good.*
- In ups and downs, *God is good.*
- In joy and in sadness, *the Lord is good.*
- In times of prosperity and even in times of need, *the Lord is good.*

O give thanks to the Lord, for God is good!

- *"For we know that all things work together for the good of those who love God, and are called according to God's purpose"* (Romans 8:28).
- *"God's steadfast love endures forever, and God's mercies are new every morning"* (Lamentations 3:23).
- Oh, that people of faith would find it within ourselves to *mind our manners*, and find reasons to be grateful in the days that are ours.

When I think of the goodness of Jesus

145

C. Anthony Hunt

And all that he's done for me
My soul cries out, Hallelujah,
I thank God for saving me!

31 - LET'S WORK WHILE WE WAIT

Be still before the LORD and wait patiently for God; do not fret when people succeed in their ways, when they carry out their wicked schemes. Refrain from anger and turn from wrath; do not fret - it leads only to evil. (Psalm 37:7-8)

Hope in the LORD and keep God's way. God will exalt you to inherit the land; when the wicked are destroyed, you will see it. (Psalm 37:34)

When thinking about and envisioning waiting – one image that comes to mind is that of sitting in a hospital emergency waiting room. As we wait, we expect that those who can help us, medical professionals, will come at the appointed time to see about us. As we wait for help to come, we may feel that there is nothing that we can do, but wait. We may feel that all that we can do is endure the pain we are experiencing until our help comes.

Likewise, there are times in our lives when we find ourselves having to wait on the Lord. As we wait, we want and expect God to come to see about us, and be our help. And we may feel that there is little that we can do besides to wait on the Lord.

Indeed, waiting on the Lord can be difficult. It has been said that waiting is the highest order of spiritual discipline. We want God to move, and move in our time, on our schedule. But God moves in God's proper and appointed time. God does not operate on your clock or mine. We find evidence of this throughout the scriptures.

- God blessed Sarah and Abraham with a son, Isaac, in God's time.

- God vindicated Joseph, in God's time.

- God delivered Israel from Egyptian slavery, in God's time.

- God sent Jesus, God's only begotten Son and our Savior, in God's time.

- God will show up, but God shows up, in God's time.

How do we know? In Psalm 34, David encouraged the people then to *"fret not because of evil-doers."* David was talking about those of his day who were succeeding in doing wrong, and trying to destroy David and God's people. And David was encouraging God's people to stay focused on the ways of God, while they waited on the Lord.

In other words, David was saying, "hold your peace while you wait, and know that God will heal the land, and you – God's people – will inherit the land."

"Don't fret", David said. So, what are we to do while we wait on the Lord?

First, we should pray while we wait. Frederick Douglass, the great abolitionist, intimated in the 19th century that there was a 20-year period when he prayed for the emancipation and freedom of his people from American slavery, but it was not until he (and they) got up and started praying with their feet and working for freedom, did change come. What praying with our feet looks like today is praying with our vote, and praying with our advocacy for social and economic justice, advocating for racial justice and police reform. God says, *"don't return evil for evil. Don't let anger and wrath overtake you."*

In other words, God is watching over us in the midst of our waiting, and it is incumbent on us to pray like everything depends on God, and work like everything depends on us.

Indeed, waiting can be difficulty. What must we do while we wait and pray for God to show up? What is our work plan for waiting? What should we be giving attention to while we wait?

Second, we should work and pray some more with our feet while we wait. Martin Luther King, Jr. intimated that "change never rolls in on the wheels of inevitability." While we wait, we must work – organize, strategize, mobilize and encourage each other. Fannie Lou Hamer, the great freedom fighter from Mississippi, intimated that there were times when she felt "sick and tired of being sick and tired", but she kept working (and working some more) while she waited for change to come.

Finally, we must hope while we wait. King also said that "hope is the refusal to give up despite insurmountable odds." In the midst of his waiting, David declared to the Lord, *"My hope is in you"* (Psalm 39:7). We are encouraged to do as David encouraged the people of his day to do, and *"hope in the Lord, and keep God's way"* (Psalm 37:34). While we wait, it's good to know that we can put our faith, trust and hope in the Lord. It's good to know that the prophet Isaiah's words are encouragement for us today –

God gives strength to the weary,
and increases the power of the weak.
Even youths grow tired and weary and faint,
and the young stumble and fall.
But they that wait on the Lord,
will renew their strength.
They will mount up with wings as eagles,
they will run and not get weary.
they will walk and not faint.
 (Isaiah 40:29-31)

32 - RESTORATION WILL COME

When the LORD restored the fortunes of Zion, we were like those who dream. Then our mouth was filled with laughter, and our tongue with shouts of joy; then it was said among the nations, "The LORD has done great things for them." The LORD has done great things for us, and we rejoiced. Restore our fortunes, O LORD, like the watercourses in the Negeb. May those who sow in tears reap with shouts of joy. Those who go out weeping, bearing the seed for sowing, shall come home with shouts of joy, carrying their sheaves.
(Psalm 126:1-6)

If we pay close attention, what we learn about God is that God desires and wills change and growth for us. Regardless of how good or bad things are, or have been in our lives, God's grace and mercy says that God desires that things will get better.

Based on our experience with God, we know that God wills – God desires and wishes to restore those aspects of our lives that are out of alignment with God's intent for us, individually and communally. That is the nature of divine restoration – that with some things that are out of place – out of order and alignment in our lives – God will put them back in order.

In this passage of scripture from Psalm 126, the psalmist looked back and reflected on two periods in his and the people's lives. The first was the times of their utter despair and destress – when all that they knew was out of alignment with God's will for them – the times that they needed God to restore them. And second, the psalmist was reflecting on the times when God showed up, stepped in, blessed and restored their lives.

Let's listen in on the psalmist's song for few moments. He declared, *"When the Lord restored the fortunes of Zion, we were like those who dream. Then our mouth was filled with laughter, and our tongue with shouts of joy"* (Psalm 126:1).

The psalmist's song of restoration should resonate with us today in light of everything we have gone through, lately. With all of the pandemic and pandemonium that has wreaked havoc in our lives, we should all be able to resonate with the psalmist's song. *"When the Lord restored the fortunes of Zion."*

With every bit of the tumult, trial and travail that has come our way, with all of the tragedy, trouble and tribulation that has met us, with all of the tough times that have confronted us – we can relate with the psalmist's song of restoration. *"When the Lord restored the fortunes of Zion."*

Let's listen in a bit more. The psalmist then declared, *"then it was said among the nations, "The LORD has done great things for them." The LORD has done great things for us, and we rejoiced. Restore our fortunes, O LORD, like the watercourses in the Negeb. May those who sow in tears reap with shouts of joy"* (Psalm 126:2b-5).

What we need to know is that we are like Zion as they languished in despair some 2900 years ago - needing restoration, and God restored them. We stand on the hopeful shoulders of those who have come before us, who knew that God was a God who would restore their fortunes. Indeed, today we stand on the hopeful shoulders of those who witnessed God bring them out of the oppressive grips of American slavery – those who experienced God bring them out of the strangle-hold of Jim Crow – those who witnessed God bring them out of economic, social and political despair.

Indeed, the same God who restored Zion, and restored other people in days past, will restore us today and tomorrow.

The promise of God for us is that restoration will come. The promise is that God's mercies are new each and every day, and God's faithfulness is great. God in Christ shows up anew to restore us, and make things new in our lives. God in Christ shows up, redeems us, restores us and saves us. Restoration will come for us.

That is why David could pray to God in Psalm 51:12, *"Lord, restore unto (us) the joy of your salvation, and uphold us with your free spirit."*

That is why the prophet Jeremiah could declare God's promises, *"for I will restore health to you, and your wounds will heal"* (Jeremiah 30:17).

Indeed, God specializes in restoration. The same God, Jehovah-rophe, who restored and healed in David's days, and restored and healed in Jeremiah's days, will heal and restore us today and tomorrow.

What do we need God to restore in our lives today– health in our bodies, peace in our minds, joy in our spirits, wholeness in our relationships? What is it that we need the Lord to step in and restore today – unity in the church, peace in our homes, justice for the oppressed, safety in our communities, accord amidst political discord? What is it that we need God to restore?

"Then our mouth was filled with laughter, and our tongue with shouts of joy" (Psalm 126:2), the psalmist declared. Whatever it is that we need to be restored, it's good to know that God specializes in restoration.

Indeed, those of us who walk by faith and not by sight walk believing that restoration will come.

"Those who go out weeping.... shall come home with shouts of joy" (Psalm 126:6), the psalmist concluded. Restoration will come. *"Weeping may endure for a night, but joy comes in the morning"* (Psalm 30:5). Restoration will come!

Jesus – the light of the world, the savior of the world, the prince of peace, joy unspeakable – will show up. Restoration will come!

33 - (GOD IS) STILL MIGHTY

"Then I thought, "To this I will appeal: the years when the Most High stretched out God's right hand. I will remember the deeds of the LORD; yes, I will remember your miracles of long ago. "I will consider all your works and meditate on all your mighty deeds." (Psalm 77:10-12)

As we make our way to Psalm 77:10-12, we find that Asaph, the psalmist, a worship leader, is contemplating and considering the ways of the Lord. Asaph is reflecting on the ways that God has been at work in his life. In a few preceding verses (Ps. 77:7-9), Asaph had prayed all night long and even expressed feelings of concern that God had forgotten, rejected and neglected him.

This message is for some of us who have felt, lately, that God, similarly, has forgotten, neglected and rejected us. This is a word for some of us who have paused at certain points throughout this year, and talked to the Lord, and asked God, "what in the world is going on in our lives?"

Hear Asaph cry out to God in his despair in Psalm 77:7-9:

> *Will the Lord reject forever? Will God never show God's favor again? Has God's unfailing love vanished forever? Has God's promise failed for all time? Has God forgotten to be merciful? Has God in anger withheld God's compassion?"*

Indeed, this is a word for some of us who are dealing with the raw reality of at points having felt, like Asaph - forgotten, forsaken, neglected and rejected, even by God.

Asaph's song serves as a reminder for us that we are not the first generation to experience pandemics of despair – pandemics of health crisis and death, pandemics of financial loss and wondering how we will make it to tomorrow.

If the truth is told, 2020 has been a year of years - a year when many of us (if not almost all of us) have shed our share of bitter tears. This has been a year where we have endured our share of pain and uncertainty, trials and adversity, difficulty and distress, sadness and sorrow, valleys and vicissitudes. And it is hard, amidst pandemic, to consider the mighty works of the Lord.

But Asaph offers us a lesson in how to have hope in despair, and how to have faith amidst doubt, as he sang in the midst of his own despair and doubt. At these junctures, when we may feel like giving up on God and ourselves, when we may feel like throwing in the towel and tapping out on life, it can help to check in on Asaph.

Asaph followed his lament, his crying out to God, by declaring to the Lord in Psalm 77:10-12:

> *"Then I thought, "To this I will appeal: the years when the Most High stretched out God's right hand. I will remember the deeds of the LORD; yes, I will remember your miracles of long ago. "I will consider all your works and meditate on all your mighty deeds."*

Asaph's song helps us to see that it is exactly at our moments of greatest despair that we need to stop – take time-out, breathe – and consider who God is, and what God has already done for us.

Asaph had sense enough to come to the conclusion that in and through all that he had endured, after all was said and done, God had stretched out God's hand and done mighty deeds in his life. The same God who had been mighty in the past, was mighty for Asaph. And the same God who was mighty for Asaph, will be mighty for you and me today and tomorrow.

God is still mighty. How many of us have taken time lately to stop, breather and consider the mighty works of the Lord? How many of us have taken time lately to meditate on the mighty deeds of God? How many of us have taken the time to consider that in and through everything we've gone through, in and through it all, God is still mighty?

How do we know that God is still mighty?

Let's take a moment to consider how God, in and through all that we have endured, has been mighty in our lives.

- God awakened us today for a brand-new day.
- God kept us through many dangers, toils and snares.
- God provided for us.
- God healed us, or somebody we know.
- God saved our souls and made us whole.

And so, in and through it all, we still have reasons to thank and praise God, and reasons to acknowledge that God is still mighty.

- Did I say that God awakened us today for a brand-new day?

- Did I say that God kept us through many dangers, toils and snares?
- Did I say that God provided for all of our needs?
- Did I say that God healed us, or somebody we know?
- Did I say that God saved our souls and made us whole?

Some of us have an Asaph praise, and we can testify that God is still mighty!

An Asaph praise - *"If it had not been for the Lord who was on our side, we don't know where we would be?"* (Psalm 124:1)

An Asaph praise – *"I've been young, and I've been old, but I've never seen the righteous forsaken, or God's seed begging for bread"* (Psalm 37:25).

An Asaph praise – *"When I look back over my life and think things over, I can truly say, I've been blessed. I've got a testimony."*

An Asaph praise - *When I think of the goodness of Jesus, and all that he's done for me, my soul cries out hallelujah. I thank God for saving me!*

God is still mighty!

34 - OPEN OUR EYES

"Be good to your servant while I live, that I may obey your word. Open my eyes that I may see wonderful things in your law. I am a stranger on earth; do not hide your commands from me." (Psalm 119:17-19)

If the truth is told, all of us really have a yearning to know what God's purpose and vision is for our lives.

Indeed, God has a vision - a preferred purpose, plan and future - for each of us. One of life's most significant challenges is to align our lives with this God's divine vision, the purpose that God has for us.

As it regards vision, there are typically two forms of hindrance to fully seeing what we need to see – *myopia and blindness.*

The first hindrance is myopia. Our vision becomes myopic when our perspectives, what we see, is limited and tunnel-focused. Many people suffer from myopia. We have tunnel-vision - we can see, but we can't fully see all that is before us. People with myopic vision can see, but we can't see all that God has in store for us - spiritually, materially, intellectually, emotionally, relationally, and as a civilization and world.

The second hindrance to complete vision is blindness. Many people are spiritually blind, where we find ourselves not only being myopic and have tunnel-vision, but we find ourselves not being able to see and sense, at all, what God's vision is for our lives.

In Psalm 119, we find the longest of all the psalms, with 176 verses. The psalm is divided into 22 stanzas that align with the 22 letters of the Hebrew alphabet. The theme throughout Psalm 119, this long-playing song, is a yearning for the people of God to fully understand and live in the word and will of God. The hope here is that the people of God - those who were walking by faith - would yearn to fully understand and live God's vision – God's purpose and plan - for their lives.

To open the third stanza of Psalm 119, in verses 17-19, the psalmist sang these lyrics -

> *"Be good to your servant while I live, that I may obey your word. Open my eyes that I may see wonderful things in your law. I am a stranger on earth; do not hide your commands from me."*

The psalmist's prayer is as appropriate and applicable for us today as it was for people of God some 2900 years ago.

"Open my eyes that I may see wonderful things in your law."

The psalmist's prayer that the Lord would open his eyes is also as appropriate and applicable for us as it was for the rhythm and blues prophets - the elements of the universe, Earth, Wind and Fire -

In 1974 - Earth, Wind and Fire - sampled a gospel sentiment in one of their popular songs - *Open Our Eyes* -

They sang -
> *Father, open our eyes,*
> *that we may see, to follow thee.*
> *Oh Lord grant us, thy lovin' peace, and let*
> *all dissension cease.*
> *Let our faith, each day increase,*

and Master - Lord please -
Open our eyes, open our eyes.

Similarly, the psalmist prayed to the Lord, *"Open my eyes that I may see wonderful things in your law."*

God knows, we need the Lord to open our eyes today –

- *that we might see more clearly how to deal with racism and sexism,*
- *see more clearly how to address economic despair and political discord,*
- *see more clearly how to deal with violence on our streets,*
- *see more clearly how to ensure that all of God's people have adequate health-care, adequate food, clean water and shelter,*
- *see more clearly how to ensure that no child is left behind,*
- *see that every one of God's children is fully educated and protected,*
- *and see more clearly how we will make it through pandemic and pandemonium.*

Yes indeed, just as rivers rage, waves batter shorelines, and lightning shreds the sky - pandemic and pandemonium have disrupted and disturbed our lives.

O that the Lord would open our eyes to God's hope and vision for our future. O that God would open our eyes to see more clearly how to love our neighbors and our enemies. O that God would open our eyes to see more clearly how to do justice, love kindness and be humbler in our daily walk.

Lord, open our eyes.

And finally, in their song, Earth, Wind and Fire offered an affirmation and praise to God:

God has given us, hills and mountains,
God has given us, level places.
God has given us, food and clothing,
given us shelter from the storm and the rain-
And all that God provided
Kept us… From the storm and the pain.

When we open our eyes, we can't help but likewise celebrate that in and through it all - God has been our shelter from the storm and the rain.

When we open our eyes, we can't help but likewise extoll the goodness of the Lord, even in difficult seasons.

- We see that God in Christ has been a very present help in our times of trouble.
- We see that God in Christ, even in this season, has continued to make ways out of no way.
- We see that God in Christ, even in this season, has been a helper and a healer, a keeper, carrier and comforter.

Our encouragement is to open our eyes, keep looking up, and keep believing that God is going to show up.

Keep looking up and keep believing that although weeping may be enduring in our lives, joy will eventually come.

Keep looking up to the hills from where our help comes – knowing that our help comes from the Lord.

35 - IT'S A DONE DEAL

I will praise you, because of what you have done. (Psalm 52:9)

By all measures, the past few days, weeks, months and years have been times of immense uncertainty in our lives. Our lives have been filled with uncertainty as to what the future holds for us... filled with uncertainty about the economy... uncertainty about our jobs (for some of us) ... uncertainty about our health... uncertainty about when COVID-19 will end... and certainly uncertainty about who will lead this nation.

There are a couple of observations that we can make about uncertainty. The first is that when we are uncertain, we have the tendency to fall into doubt. When we are uncertain, we tend to doubt whether the things that may have appeared to be certain are certain for us at all. When we are uncertain, we tend to harbor doubt as to whether situations and circumstances are the way we think they ought to be.

And a second observation is that the result of our doubts is our worries. We begin to worry. We worry about things at home. We worry about our children. We worry about our husband or wife. We worry about our boyfriend or girlfriend. We worry about our job. We worry about neighbors. Our lives are filled with worry.

Certainly, there are some problems that are too big for us... some situations that are too difficult and complicated for us to handle. Amidst this reality, people today need something and somebody in which to place our confidence and trust. We need something and somebody in which to find certainty amidst uncertainty. In what and in whom can we can put our faith and trust?

For a prescriptive to our uncertainty, we go to Psalm 52:9. Hear these words of comfort, encouragement and praise from David: *"(Lord) I will praise you forever, for what you have done."*

As we reflect on David's words, we recall that he experienced a multitude of ups and downs in his life. A shepherd boy in his youth, David would eventually be led into battle with a Philistine giant, named Goliath. David defeated Goliath, and went on to be blessed by God to become the king of Israel.

But despite his success, David continued to experience difficulties in his life and walk with God. We witness David's predicaments throughout the many psalms that he wrote:

On one account he would sing:

"Lord, because your lovingkindness is better than life, I will praise you" (Psalm 63:3).

Then he would be led to sing:

"Lord, have mercy on me according to your lovingkindness" (Psalm 51:1).

On another occasion David sang:

"I will bless the Lord at all times; God's praise shall continually be in my mouth" (Psalm 34:1).

And the next moment he asked:

"My God, my God why have forsaken me?" (Psalm 22:1).

In David's songs, we can hear and sense the ups and downs of his life. David went through some things.

- For every victory, there was a vicissitude.
- For every triumph, there was a trial.
- For every battle won, there was a bitter defeat.
- For every sign of David's faithfulness, there was a symbol of existential despair.

And aren't we often like David?

- For all the times that we are faithful to God, aren't there just as many moments that we find ourselves lacking faith?
- For every time that we are certain of God's presence, aren't there just as many instances of uncertainty and wonder for us?
- For all the times when we rise to the occasion in life without any doubt or fear, aren't there just as many moments when we are filled with doubt in our hearts and minds.

David declared:

"Lord, I will praise you forever, because of what you have done."

Another translation says: *"Lord, I will praise you, for you did it."*

"I will praise you, because of what you have done." "Lord, you did it."

The good news is that because of what God has already done, and is doing, we know that with whatever we may need tomorrow, it is a "done deal."

And so – whatever we may need, God will do it for us. Healing for our bodies – done. Provision for our needs – done. Peace for our minds – done. Hope to run on – done. Salvation for our souls – done. *It's a done deal!*

36 - HOPE SINGS!

By the rivers of Babylon, we sat and wept when we remembered Zion. There on the poplars we hung our harps, for there our captors asked us for songs, our tormentors demanded songs of joy; they said, "Sing us one of the songs of Zion!" How can we sing the songs of the LORD while in a foreign land? If I forget you, Jerusalem, may my right hand forget its skill. May my tongue cling to the roof of my mouth if I do not remember you, if I do not consider Jerusalem my highest joy. (Psalm 137:1-6)

In Psalm 137, we find ourselves at the place of a depiction of the predicament of the Israelites who found themselves in exile by the rivers in Babylon. Here the Israelites were, trapped in bondage... trapped in alienation and exile in a strange land... trapped and cut off from all that had been familiar to them - their land, their families and their song.

And here, in this strange-land situation, their Babylonian captors asked the people of Israel – these people of faith - to sing one of their songs of Zion. In their exile, they were provoked and prodded by their captors to sing their song. And in their desperation, the Israelites' response was in a question, *"How do we sing the Lord's song in a strange land?"*

The Israelites understandably found themselves in no mood to sing. How were they supposed to sing in the midst of adversity? How were they supposed to sing amidst exile, separation and alienation? They were in no mood to sing ... trouble all around them... no hope and no joy. *How were they supposed to sing the Lord's song?*

And so, perhaps, it could help us to take a moment to pause and reflect on who we are in light of the songs we need to sing today. If there is anything that people of the African Diaspora share in common, it is that we are a singing people. This is to say that if there is any one thing that defines African people, it is our ability and willingness to sing. This has been one of our stamps, one of our marks. We are a singing people.

In 1903, renowned sociologist W.E.B. DuBois, in his classic book, *The Souls of Black Folk*, shared that black people have offered three significant, indelible gifts to American life as a whole – *(1) the gift of the sweat and brawn; (2) the gift of the spirit; and (3) the gift of the song and story.*

This is to say, that when African people first arrived on America's shores in the port of Jamestown in 1619, over 400 years ago – they came with a song. African persons came to these shores under various circumstances, and invariably brought with them a song, and had to keep singing. Those who would be enslaved would sing, *"Nobody knows the trouble I've seen. Nobody knows my sorrow."* They'd sing *"Swing Low, Sweet Chariot... Comin' for to carry me home."* They'd sing to the Lord, *"Cum Bah Yah, Dear Lord"*.

We are a people of the song – a people of the rhythm - a people of the beat - a people who sing. Whether in the church or at the party, we have had a song to sing. Whether in the great cathedrals of the land or the grandest of concert halls, it has been well-known that African peoples are people of the song.

What is impressive in travels to the various corners of the earth is that African people - wherever we are physically located - and whatever our lot – we are a singing people. Whether in Mutare, Zimbabwe, in Cape Town, South Africa, or in Sierra Leone on the western shores of the African continent - it is evident that we are a singing people. In the Caribbean, in Central and South America, or in any neighborhood – wherever we reside in the United States - it is clear that African people are a singing people.

Indeed, whoever we are, and from wherever we've come around the globe, we have arrived on these shores with a song. And it's really our native song - whatever it is - that has kept us, and will keep us in the days ahead.

In 1975, the soul singing prophets, Earth, Wind and Fire recorded a song that encouraged people to "Sing a Song":

When you feel down and out…
Sing a song…It'll make your day…
Here's a time to shout…
Sing a song… It'll make a way.
Sometimes it's hard to care…
Sing a song…It'll make your day…
A smile so hard to bear…
Sing a song… It'll make a way.

We hear Earth, Wind and Fire, but we know that it's not always easy to sing a song. Indeed, the turbulent, tempestuous, tumultuous and often troubling nature of contemporary times can lead us to realize how difficult it can be to sing, and keep singing a song. How do we keep singing… keep worshipping… keep praising the Lord… and keep trusting and hoping in Jesus in the midst of today's adversity?

How do we sing in the midst of abject poverty, and virulent racism and sexism? How do we sing in the midst of suffering and sickness? How can we sing amidst violence and death, where too many young people are dying on our streets? *How do we sing the Lord's song in these strange-land situations?*

I've discovered that it's easy to sing when life is rosy and cozy. It's not hard to sing when the bills are paid, and good health abounds. It's not difficult to sing amidst comfort and convenience. *But how do we sing the Lord's song in strange-land situations?*

The true challenge of singing comes amidst of the "strange-land" situations of life. The challenge of singing comes when the nights are darkest, and even the days are dim, when there is little money in the bank... when it seems that loved ones have forsaken us... when it seems that we've done all that we can do to stand.

This is why we need to take time every now and then to be reminded of the importance of our perpetual song. We will all face strange-land situations in life. There will be times for all of us when we sit, as the Israelites sat, beside the proverbial "rivers of Babylon."

There will be times when we feel separated and segregated from God, and from one another. All of us will experience times of loneliness and lostness, times of alienation and anxiety, and times of desperation and disillusionment. It is in our strange land situations – "by the rivers of Babylon" - that it is most important to keep singing.

And we are encouraged to know that it's all right to ask, as did the Israelites, the question, *"How can we sing God's song."* It's all right to talk to the Lord, and ask God the question. For to ask the question indicates that we are still in conversation with the Lord. It indicates that we are still seeking and searching for the Lord to help us sing even though we may not feel like singing.

To ask the question *"How do we sing?"* is to acknowledge - at the depths of our souls - that we may be bent, but we are not yet broken. It is to recognize that we may be hurting, but we know that healing is possible. We may feel helpless, but we know that if we hold on – our help is on the way. It's all right to ask the question, *"How do we keep singing the Lord's song?"*

The real problem comes not in asking the question, *"How do we sing?"* The real problem comes when we stop singing altogether. The real problem comes when we feel that there is no use in singing. The real faith predicament lies at the moment when we sense that all hope is gone, and that we may as well throw in the towel, give up and stop singing. The problem really is evident when we stop singing the Lord's song.

The Israelites were asked by their Babylonian captors to sing their song. And so, eventually, they sang. For they knew that in their captivity and in their difficulty, it would be their song that would keep and carry them. They knew that God would show up in a song. They knew that the Spirit would descend in a song. They knew that the melody needed to linger to keep them alive and give them hope.

And it is hope that gives us the strength and courage to sing through adversity and amidst our adversaries. *Hope sings!*

We are encouraged today to keep singing... Indeed, if there is anything that we who are African Americans have learned during our more than 400 years on these American shores, it is that we have to keep singing. Yes, pandemic and pandemonium continue to plague many of our people – but we have to keep singing. Drugs are poisoning many of our people – but we have to keep singing. Guns and violence are afflicting our communities – but we need to keep singing.

Those who sang the blues, like Billie Holiday, Bessie Smith and B.B King were really helping us understand that whatever the strange-land situations… whatever the circumstances… whatever the predicaments we find ourselves in - we have to keep singing. Whatever blows have been directed at us, or will come our way - we need to keep singing.

Hope sings!

It's good that persons of faith like Thomas Dorsey, Charles Tindley, Mattie Moss Clark, Shirley Caesar and James Cleveland were so inspired to take the blues and turn it into Gospel Music. They knew that despite the blues, despite the strange-land situations, it was important to keep singing.

And so, Charles Tindley sang:

> *When the storms of life are raging*
> *(Lord) stand by me…*
> *When the storms of life are raging*
> *(Lord) stand by me…*
> *When the world is tossing me*
> *Like a ship upon the sea*
> *Thou who rulest wind and water*
> *(Lord) stand by me.*

Hope sings!

And Thomas Dorsey sang:

> *Precious Lord ...Take my hand*
> *Lead me on ...Let me stand.*
> *I am tired ... I am weak ... I am worn.*
> *Through the storm ... through the night*
> *Lead me on ... to the light*
> *Take my hand ... Precious Lord*
> *Lead me home.*

Hope sings!

And then James Cleveland came along years later and sang:
I don't feel no ways tired
I've come too far from where I started from
Nobody told me that the road would be easy
I don't believe (God) brought (us) this far to leave (us).

We're reminded and encouraged that in and through it all, hope sings!

- We can keep singing because we know that *there's a balm in Gilead to make the wounded whole, and heal the sin-sick soul.*
- We can keep singing because we know that *over our heads, there's music in the air (and there must be a God somewhere).*
- We keep singing because we know that in our song, the Spirit will descend and God is preparing to bless us.

Hope sings!

> *My hope is built on nothing less*
> *Than Jesus' blood and righteousness.*
> *I dare not trust the sweetest frame*
> *But wholly lean in Jesus's name.*
> *On Christ the solid Rock I stand*
> *All other ground is sinking sand.*
> *All other ground is sinking sand!*
> *(Edward Mote)*

ABOUT THE AUTHOR

A native of Washington D.C., Rev. Dr. C. Anthony Hunt is the Senior Pastor of Epworth Chapel United Methodist Church in Baltimore, MD, and is Professor of Systematic, Moral and Practical Theology and Permanent Dunning Distinguished Lecturer at the Ecumenical Institute of Theology, St. Mary's Seminary and University in Baltimore. He also teaches at Wesley Theological Seminary in Washington, DC, United Theological Seminary in Dayton, OH, and the Graduate Theological Foundation in Oklahoma City, OK, where he is a Faculty Fellow and the E. Franklin Frazier Professor of African-American Studies.

A graduate of the University of Maryland, he holds advanced degrees from Troy State University, Wesley Theological Seminary and the Graduate Theological Foundation. Additionally, he has completed post-graduate studies at the Center of Theological Inquiry, Princeton, NJ; the University of Oxford, UK; St. Mary's Seminary and University, Baltimore, MD; Bethel University, St. Paul, MN; and the Institute of Certified Professional Managers, James Madison University, Harrisonburg, Va. He is an inductee in the Rev. Dr. Martin Luther King, Jr. International Board of Preachers at Morehouse College, Atlanta, GA.

He is the author of thirteen other books including, *Holding on to Hope: Essays, Sermons and Prayers on Religion and Race, vol. 4* (2020); *Songs for the Seasons: Sermons on the Psalms, vol. 2* (2020); *I've Seen the Promised Land: Martin Luther King, Jr. and the 21ˢᵗ Century Quest for the Beloved Community* (2020); and *Come Go with Me: Howard Thurman and a Gospel of Radical Inclusivity* (2019); and over 200 articles, chapters and academic papers on matters pertaining to religion and society.

Made in the USA
Middletown, DE
16 June 2021